SINGING IN THE
MOMENT

SINGING IN THE MOMENT

A choir director's notes on life, learning and contentment.

POOGIE
THE PUP

Publishing

Dr. Joel Plaag

First paperback edition August 2021

ISBN: 978-1-7373518-0-1
E-book ISBN: 978-1-7373518-1-8

Published by Poogie the Pup Publishing
www.joelplaag.cc
.

TABLE OF CONTENTS

PROLOGUE

There's something to be said for going back in time to tell oneself how to handle "life stuff." Every week, I write notes to my choir. First, they were formal "Choir Notes." They talked about aspects of rehearsal or notes about the various ideas portrayed in a piece of music.

As time wore on, I wanted to write more than just the music. After all, isn't music a reflection of life? Can't we make connections through music into life lessons? Isn't rehearsing a choir, singing in a choir, and directing a choir a microcosm for the life lessons we learn in the "outside" world?

This book is not about choir. It's just written by someone who works with choirs.

In 2006, I finished my doctorate in music, writing a thesis about movement theory and conducting. I knew

I wanted to write about directing choirs, but I also wanted to help others. "Write about getting your mind right," one friend said.

I put the idea of writing for fun out of my head. I got involved teaching. I led a community chorus, taught courses, and worked at a college.

Then I lost my job. I moved home, no longer surrounded by old friends, or comforted by a career that had seemed so certain. In short, I had to start over. I found an apartment, got a job, and started the process of moving on.

But something else happened during that time: I began to pray.

I asked God, "Put me where You need me most." He placed me back in a former church position. I was reacquainted with friends from more than ten years earlier. A new sense of peace began to develop, and, for the first time in a long time, I gave myself permission to write again.

I first became acquainted with the idea of letters to the choir from Robert Shaw's biography, *Dear People*. Shaw wrote funny, witty letters describing what he wanted from the choir.

As I worked with volunteer singers, I realized our singers come to rehearsal filled with the week's situations and problems. Yet for a few hours a week, I get to offer a brief respite from the world.

Prologue

Every week I write to the choir on Mondays in what I call "Choir Notes." Some notes are functional, showing musical nuances or revealing rehearsal orders or seating charts. Others are funny reminders of what we do. Some have very little to do with music, since choral music is made by human beings that need healing, self-love, and a relationship with the Divine Creator. These non-musical "Notes" make up this book.

Though sometimes I refer to musical ideas, hopefully my musical forays are brief and non-technical.

Ultimately, I hope my desire to help others through telling stories can allow us all to live better in harmony on this little planet that we all have to share.

I hope you find some of the love, wonder, and excitement on reading these notes as I found in creating them.

Singing in the Moment

SINGING IN THE MOMENT

A choir director's notes on life, learning and contentment.

Singing in the Moment

NOTE #1

HAVE A PLAN. FEEL FREE TO IGNORE IT

As a new choir director, especially at my first church, I walked into the rehearsal room about an hour before it started. I took all the anthems, looked at them, and played through them. When the choir came in, we practiced them in order of appearance. This Sunday's anthem was first, then the next Sunday, and the next, and so on.

Right away I noticed something – extreme boredom.

Now to be fair, this was my first church choir. Actually, it was my first *choir*. I was a junior in college and looking forward to graduate school and conducting great major works with a trusty baton, so I never really worried about what I would be rehearsing. (That didn't turn out the way I planned.)

I'd never dreamed of having an order of rehearsing – or having an order for anything else for that matter. I just kind of moved through what I thought were the most important parts of the rehearsal and left the rest to God. I did this in my day too – just floated along pretending everything was ok. This all worked great for me until something unexpected happened; then it all backfired. I couldn't get the work done and I couldn't move forward.

Rehearsal plans aren't just in rehearsals; they are in life too. My husband and I repeatedly ask each other, "What are you going to do today?" There is always a list of things to do: walk the dogs, get food, cook, clean, fix something, work on a project, go to work, invite someone over, play cards, go to sleep, repeat.

When the order of the day, much like the order of rehearsal, changes drastically, I tell someone. In the choir's case, I stand up and say, "I'm about to go against the rehearsal order." (I used to ask if anyone wanted to object but stopped because the jokes began and the rehearsal would descend into chaos.) Usually someone in the Tenor section snickered "ooooo."

Why is it always the Tenors?

For a long time, I lived in a vacuum. My choices affected only me, and my consequences only involved me. But in a true community, changes in plans involve at least one other person.

A plan works for other events beside rehearsals. In a study from the *British Journal of Health Psychology,* researchers measured 248 adults on their exercise frequency. The group was required to keep track of how often they exercised. The adults were divided into three groups, a control group who were asked to read three paragraphs of a novel, a motivation group who read a pamphlet about the benefits of exercise, and an intention group, who also read the motivational pamphlet as well as formulated a plan for when and where they would exercise.

After two weeks, the results came in. The first two groups, the control and motivation groups, exercised about the same amount of time. The third group, however, had more than 90% still exercising at least once per week! A specific plan helped them stick to their goals of exercising.

So, for heaven's sake, create a plan. Stick to it. And if you can't stay on it, tell someone.

Maybe they'll have a better idea.

NOTE #2

HOLD FAST TO THE TREE

One of my friends, commenting on orchestra conductor Ricardo Muti, was amazed at the man's stance.

"He doesn't move!" he said. "He stays so grounded, like a tree."

Watching this great conductor practice his craft, I too was moved by the pull of his leadership. I watched as he evoked sound and emotion out of choirs and orchestras, all with the wave of his hands. My friend's observation was right; Muti didn't move his feet. He stayed planted on the podium, a bulwark of musical leadership.

When I conduct, I still think of this model. I ground myself, plant my feet firmly, keep my ribcage tall, breathe low, and gesture to reflect how the sound should be in my mind's ear. Like a tree, both in conducting and in my spiritual life, I try to stay grounded.

These days a tree stands guard in front of my home. Its branches are long, stretching high above, shadowing a good portion of the house. After having it trimmed a few years ago, it looks now as a storybook caricature of a tree.

Trees like this are fed through overhanging leaves above and roots below which burrow through the soil to create a strong anchor. They billow in breezes and bend. Though small branches break, the tree endures year after year. Today that tree continues growing, shading people and grass underneath, stopping too much water from reaching the earth, and adapting to the fall or spring so the ground stays warmer or cooler.

As I was on my hands and knees creating little tunnels through the exposed roots for landscape wiring, I realized that it isn't just the branches that connect the tree, it's the soil. The vaster the root network, the better it can receive water and minerals; and the harder it is to uproot.

Staying grounded and anchored requires two things. First, it requires a strong, wide root system. For a tree, this develops over time into nutrient-collecting and water-gathering tendrils. For Muti, it's a firm stance. For us, it's a sense of balance, relaxation, and vitality.

Like the tree, I require a good place to anchor. In my yard the heavy, thick clay provides weight and connection to the roots and keeps them from moving far.

Except sometimes trees do grow in bad soil. The formidable, unforgiving clay around my house doesn't hold water, has few nutrients, and fewer minerals. Yet the oak tree in the front grows just the same. In fact, there are numerous oak trees just on my street alone.

What is my anchor system if I'm in bad soil? It is my friends, my family, God, a sense of purpose, and a feeling of usefulness. We're not always placed in perfect growing soil. Our connections to the ground may be tenuous, but we do have one thing: we have that life force flowing through us, encouraging us to grow.

How do we remain grounded?

1. We can enjoy the work with other people. Start a new health routine. Take a new class. Do it with others.
2. We can take time to appreciate the moments. Appreciate the things that we have and the things we make. Too often I sat back and said "I'll be happy with this when…" instead of enjoying what is happening right now.
3. We can take our time. Take a break before getting flustered or burnt out.
4. We can practice self-care. No one else will stop us to remind us to rest or eat. No one else will take care of us as well as we can.

5. We can stay active. I mow, ride my bicycle, walk, and of course I fix a lot of things around the house. An active body keeps an active mind.
6. We can enjoy the mundane. Dance in the grocery store, listen to music instead of the news, connect with friends, read outside, write. We can do those things that bring happiness.
7. We can be compassionate. Compassion comes from the word *compati*, which means "suffer with." Though we may not experience pain with others, we can walk through their pain with them just with our presence.

There's a song based on Proverbs 3:18, *Etz Chayim hi*, which is sung as the Torah is put away. In a sad, mournful melody, the doors to the Ark are closed while these words are sung:

> *It is a tree of life for those who hold fast to it,*
> *and all its supporters are happy. Its ways*
> *are ways of pleasantness, and all its paths*
> *are peace.*

The text calls to us to grow through scripture, prayer, song, and work. At the end of the day, like the tree, we must encourage our own growth, even in the most unfertile, inhospitable soil.

Reach out. Find your network. And grow.

NOTE #3

WALK DOWN THE HALLWAY

My dog Teddy, at nearly 100 pounds of white, Great-Pyrenees fur, is afraid of the hallway.

He didn't start out that way. When we first adopted him, Teddy didn't give a second thought to it. Running back and forth with our smaller dog, Freckles, twice-rejected Teddy is happy to finally have a forever home.

About a year ago, Freckles started chewing on himself, so we had to put a cone on his head. Not mindful of the cone or the extra space needed to go down the hallway, he frequently bumped into the wall and dragged the cone. As he dragged, it made an agonizing "cccHHHHHHHH" as he quickly ran for the garage door, where the leashes and the great outside walk waited for him. My husband Michael and I laughed at Freckles' boldness.

Teddy didn't like that noise. It really spooked him, so he avoided it as best he could. Worried about hearing the dragging cone, Teddy began to study the hallway in anticipation of that horrible sound.

First, he looked at the hallway. Next, he tenderly steped one furry paw into the hallway, searching with his giant face to see if the cone is still there. Then he runs. In a flash, he bolts down the slippery laminate floor. Sometimes he had no problems. Often, though, he tripped over his feet, causing him to run faster.

Teddy must decide. Should he go down the scary, scary hallway? Should he ignore the happy sounds of one of his owners, waiting to feed or pet him from another room?

The perplexity is on his face when he looks down the scary hallway. But then he finds a way. It took a while at first; only with a leash, then after being called repeatedly, and now, he confidently walks down without much thought.

In some ways, watching Teddy reminds me of my own fears. Maybe it's not an actual hallway, but I have "hallways" that are just as real as Teddy's. Like Teddy, my idea is to get through as fast as possible.

We all have hallways to walk down. It may be ending a friendship that's outgrown its time. It may be saying no to an abusive family member. Maybe it's just not getting another bag of cookies. Scary, scary hallways keep us from doing the right thing. They allow others to take our power. They allow us to be crushed by the everyday winds that blow our way.

We have help. No one must walk scary, scary hallways alone. Usually waiting at the other end is a friend, a spouse, or in Teddy's case, an owner to walk down the hallway. Of course, God cheers us on as we take that first step, too.

Today, like every day, Teddy walked down the hallway, and each time he does it, he gets a little braver. Eventually, it became no big deal.

I used to suffer from stage fright. When I sang, my brow would furl, and my posture collapsed. For singers, a collapsed rib cage means poor breath support, and poor singing technique.

One day my voice teacher asked me in a rather pointed tone, "You're allowing yourself to get in the way of your singing. Why do you do that?"

I couldn't give him an answer. I never questioned the reality of that fear. I never stopped to consider that stage fright might not be inevitable. I felt I had no control over it.

My teacher asked me to rehearse all the technical parts of my singing until they were automatic. He wanted me to use my technique as a go-to, so that when I was afraid, I did not relapse into old behaviors. If I missed notes or words, it was fine, but I always needed to make sure I created a good tone.

Shortly after that, I started to outgrow the fear. I learned that if I accept certain things about myself like stage fright as always true, I will never outgrow them. It would bar me from moving forward, just like Teddy's hallway.

Like my early form of stage fright, I feel fear when I play a keyboard. As a fledgling organist, I'd practiced an arrangement of *Lasst Uns Erfreuen* for months. This short, two-page response is a staple of our weekly services and is about a full minute of terror. The second page is entirely handwritten and hard to read. It's a true challenge for a beginner organist like me.

I've played the organ in church before, but this was different. My friend the organist was depending on me, and I couldn't let her down. As the moment approached, I reminded myself: *I can do this.*

I walked down the hallway. I played my best, and for all those struggles, no one noticed the terror I experienced over these thirty seconds of the worship service. This was a personal struggle, played out in a drama for one.

When I'm sitting at a keyboard instrument the fear strikes me breathless, powerless, and useless. As time went on, the world didn't come apart when I missed a note or two. In fact, my love for music eventually overshadowed my fear of playing.

My comfort level with the pedals improved and I found notes that used to be a mystery. Without this terrifying ordeal, I never would have sat down at the organ, day after day, working towards Sunday morning. I discovered a new appreciation for the organist's quiet reassuring presence, leading worship and engaging us to be singers.

If we have a goal to achieve, we learn to ignore the fear and doubt. The trick isn't just playing the instrument or singing – it's ignoring those negative voices.

The *Inner Game of Music* refers to this as the "Two Games." The "outer" game has challenges and ways to overcome those challenges. These are the things that we learn and must do, such as play the instrument in a concert, catch the ball in a baseball game, or kick a field goal with everyone watching. The "inner" game involves roadblocks in the mind. Barry Green defines these mental obstacles as "lapses of concentration, nervousness, and self-doubt." He goes on to say that the inner game strongly influences and is "very often the deciding factor between success… and failure."

One of the ways I win in my inner game is to ask God.

When I woke up this morning, I asked God to be my conductor; leading me to do what He would have me do, and giving me the courage to do my part, even if that means just showing up.

When I ask for assistance from the Source of Peace, it means quieting the self-doubt of my ego so that I can get my job done; that I serve God by leaving my own internal battle out of the equation.

When I sing, play the piano, conduct a choir, give a sermon, or do any sort of public task, I feel a little flutter each time. Today I don't listen as much to it. Instead, I focus on the technique, the project, and the work at hand.

I remind myself I have a job to do.

Eventually, like Teddy in the hallway, I got over my fear because there was something I needed to do. Like Teddy, I became comfortable with my hallway.

NOTE #4

TAKE THE COMPLIMENT

G ood rehearsal," someone might say.
If you only knew, I think to myself.
I spent years saying this when someone said something nice to me. Anything at all would set this statement off in my head. I thought I was being "humble." Humility means learning to think of yourself as small, right?

Then I learned to just say thank you and shut up. By showing this supposed "humility," I was drawing attention to it.

> *Look how humble I can be for you by*
> *downplaying your compliment.*

Note #4

*My opinion of how rotten I am is better than
yours!*

*My failings are far more important than
anything you could ever see.*

Seems humble enough.

Everyone gets to have whatever opinion they want –
whether about their jeans, their politics, their musical
choices, or their cars. Sometimes I have strong opinions.
Compliments? Those are awful.

I learned a simple phrase from an old friend.

"I appreciate that," he'd say.

Hardy was a Vietnam veteran who used to squat
down close to the ground when he would talk to others.
He spoke often of his two German shepherds, his Mazda
Miata, and a daughter who was the light of his life. He
lit the room up like a great fire of joy when he entered.

"Bless you!" he'd bellow, enthusiastically. After this
standard greeting, he'd bow, and I always felt the
greatest warmth in those greetings. His enthusiasm and
his smile greeted me as sincerely as his phrase.

When a compliment was made to him, he'd just
respond. "I appreciate that."

It was so simple. He knew that the person
complimenting him meant it sincerely and genuinely.

With a twinkle in his eye, partially with love and reverence, he'd utter that phrase.

On the other hand, when I hear a compliment, I point out the flaws in my technique. I assume they don't know, so I tell them. When someone says something nice, I essentially say they're mistaken.

But my friend didn't do that. He just said those words:

"I appreciate that."

Conversation over. We moved on.

One summer, my husband bought me a chop saw, and along with a pocket jig and some screws, together we created a bookcase. It filled the entire wall, was drilled into the studs, and looked like it had always been there. It was a fun project that covered an awkward part of the front room where the ceiling is low. I added a new plug, transformer and two puck lights to highlight some of the large African art displayed on the shelves.

Unfortunately, there are problems. The trim isn't perfect. If I look closely, I can see slight deviations on the sides. The drywall patch, where I ran electrical wire, is noticeable. The shelves in the two side panels (which I did by myself) aren't perfectly even. The pocket holes are sometimes exposed. Yet if I'm not looking for these flaws, I never see them.

It's still my first bookcase.

When someone notices the bookcase, they are usually impressed and I want to tell them, "No, it's my first one. Look how the shelves don't line up; the trim isn't perfectly straight; there is a splotch of red paint where we were going to paint the bookcase red, and then thought better of it."

I keep my mouth shut about these insecurities, and instead say, "I appreciate that."

In Kat Boogaard's article "4 Ways Confident People Accept a Compliment (That Aren't Cocky)," she says that confident people take compliments to heart!

A few other traps of supposed "humility" need to be avoided. Shifting the spotlight, where we try to tell the other person another compliment, can seem insincere. Also, it's important not to argue about the compliment, and, most importantly, say thank you!

Take heart, understand that compliments can be uncomfortable, don't try to get into a complimentary tennis match, and say thanks! Or, like my Vietnam Veteran friend, respond with "I appreciate that."

The monster of self-loathing, perfectionism and "detail-oriented" delusion can be contained by not voicing self-criticism when another person is complimenting. Accept the compliment, and don't mistake humiliation for humility.

NOTE #5

LEARN THEIR LANGUAGE OR QUIT TALKING

She was incorrigible.

As the choir director in a small town, I conducted a community chorus that was tasked with singing at the local historical society. We had to perform outside in the rain, and it didn't just rain that day, it poured! During a short pause in the rain, almost everyone in the choir was there, so with more rain threatening our small event, we sang early.

As we finished, my then-boss's wife came up to me, screaming. Though we all could have waited in the rain for her, the rest of the choir had bothered to come a little early to practice one more time. With the gathering storm and wind in the background, the woman shook her finger as she berated me, questioned my lineage, and took great offense that we started (and finished) without her.

I explained that everyone else was there; the storm was approaching, and we needed to sing, but she was so angry. She kept screaming, telling me what a horrible person I was. I said nothing; after all, she was my boss's wife. The other choristers, watching this woman yell at me, looked aghast. I too was a volunteer, not paid at all for doing this.

If I had retaliated, what could happen? Maybe another trip to see her husband, my boss? One more threat of ending my fledgling academic career? Another veiled threat of termination, leaving my friends, and disengaging from the comfortable life I made? Should I just stand there, nod, and go on?

Would the woman have ever listened?

I said nothing.

With all the threats and insinuations, her opinion about me didn't matter. For emotional people like that, it doesn't exist. Besides, I've been screamed at before.

Who really spoke louder?

There is a wonderful poem, the "Desiderata," by Max Ehrmann:

> *Go placidly amid the noise and the haste and*
> *remember what peace there may be in*
> *silence.*

At the end of the day, when we stop engaging people who have already made up their mind, we use the loudest voice of all: silence. We choose to say, "your opinion matters less to me than my own."

Family relationship psychologist Dr. Magdalena Battles reminds us that "When someone is constantly yelling at you in life, they are displaying emotional tyranny over you." Tyranny usually exists out of fear. Is that how I want to relate to other people?

Emotional tyranny can't be looked at as a dialogue, and simply agreeing with the yeller doesn't stop it. When another person has taken offense, it doesn't mean they hope I can see the error of my ways and fix whatever ails them. They are meant to upset the other person and show a power play.

Unfortunately, I used to yell a lot. I learned this skill during my twenties. I saw it in teachers, professors, doctors, and family members. Say what the other person *should* do. Tell them they must agree with me. Use my clout as best as I can to belittle the other person's behavior and perspective. Finally, give them a choice, to comply with my will, *or else*.

What a horrible thing to do to someone! The result might be compliance, but the cost is respect from the other person. In the case with the woman at the historical society, my respect for her diminished to nothing.

Some people just want to be heard. Sometimes, like in this case, it's anger. Sometimes it's self-righteousness; other times it's cruelty. It doesn't matter if the argument is good, or worthwhile, or if I am right.

Here are some tips to deal with a yeller:

1. Stay calm. "Remember what peace there may be in silence," says the *Desiderata.* Some of the most powerful words I have ever spoken were no words at all.

2. Assess the situation. Am I really at fault? Did I do this out of malice? Do I care, or should I just walk away?

3. Stay decidedly neutral. I used to agree with the yeller to stop the screaming because I was frightened. In time, it led to more yelling.

4. Calmly address the yelling, using "I" statements. Once I had a dean that insisted on screaming at me regularly. One day I addressed this, asking why he was yelling at me. Unfortunately, it caused more yelling.

5. Walk away. You never, ever, ever deserve to be belittled, or screamed at by another person. The lady on the street who screamed at me because my dogs walked across her yard is ignored. The random man who yelled at me for taking his parking spot? Ignored.

6. Give the person time to cool off and address the behavior at another time. Once I had a church member scream at me over the phone and hang up in anger. After a couple of days, I saw him. Asking him to a private conference in a corner, I expressed to him that I did not appreciate him yelling at me, and I found that tone unacceptable. He immediately apologized and has never done it again.

Sometimes people have no idea that they are acting in an unacceptable manner because they don't know any better. This may be the only way they have seen to deal with frustration or negative issues. Sometimes it just takes us telling them not to do that to open their eyes and help them see how to handle these negative feelings better. We can show compassion and empathy to some extent, but if they are unwilling to alter an unacceptable behavior, we always have the right to walk away. In fact, it is our responsibility to ourselves to do so.

NOTE #6

LOOK UP

It was eight hours later. I drove through the rain and across the entire state of Texas.

I have been to Marfa before, but this time was different. I took a different route, and along the way encountered rain in the desert. In fact, during the week I was there, I was amazed at how much it rained. By Houston standards it wasn't a lot, but the rain, after short deluges, would run across the roads, down through washes, and across the normally arid landscape.

After all that driving, I finally swept like a tumbleweed into the little town. On a cold night in September, I had finally arrived at a writing retreat in Marfa.

Marfa is a small town where about 2000 people call this place home. The place is dotted by ranchers, border patrol, lots of artists and now, unfortunately, real estate investors. In 1974 minimalist Donald Judd made Marfa his home and until his death, created sculptures and works that fill this town. It's quirky, full of shops, restaurants, tourists and other artists. The first time I ever attended a poetry reading was in the theater there.

In the middle of the pandemic and far from home, I packed as though I was camping in the wilderness. I brought all my food so that I wouldn't need to visit restaurants. I brought a fan to blot out the sound of the late-night train, and I brought cleaning supplies to thoroughly disinfect the room.

After moving into my room and cooking my first dinner over the supplied hotplate, I decided to take a walk in the brisk night air. Unlike in Houston, where light occludes all but the brightest stars, tonight I looked up on this clear, cold night and marveled at the closeness of each dot above. These stars were different, I thought as I stood outside the local hotel on the busiest intersection of town. They were not just brighter, they seemed to *invade* the night sky. Though the blazing blackness above me seemed to crush the few lights present in the little town, that same blackness carried an onslaught of stars, millions of miles away.

I'm drawn into the remoteness of West Texas. It reminds me of the awesomeness of the universe, the smallness of our own planet, and my own total insignificance. Standing in downtown, halfway between the blinking yellow light and the dramatic, nineteenth-century courthouse, the big dipper seems so much closer.

They are just stars, yes. Stars appear each night, and they occur with some regularity. In this place, they seem to reach out nearly to the touch. They *mean* something here, like wishes are louder and navigational guidance more pronounced.

Maybe it's that way with God. In the darkest of darkness, God speaks loudest, guiding us onward, helping us to discern what our specific role must be.

After all, there are bright stars guiding the way.

How often have we looked up and wondered "why am I here, in this place?"

Then I heard the theory of the Great Hand. Though I don't subscribe to the Calvinist idea that the world and all that is in it is pre-ordained, and that we carry out a predetermined role, I do believe each of us has a purpose. What does scripture tell us about that purpose: to seek justice, love mercy, and walk humbly with (our) God. (Micah 6:8)

In my own life, when I wonder why I moved to a certain place, a lesson was present too. In one place, I learned that I could connect with groups of people to make volunteer choirs. In another, I learned that I needed to go deep within myself to find God. In another, I found that I had piano skills and just lacked confidence. Next, I needed to grow: to learn the organ, lead worship, and grow comfortable in my spiritual practices. Now I can put all these skills to good use: rehearsing choirs, playing the organ, talking in front of others, leading through prayer, and connecting.

When I looked back at the past twenty years, I see that when I refused to grow, situations presented themselves forcing me to move forward.

Every decision, every movement we make leads us to this exact moment in time. Sometimes it seems like things just happen to us, but when we go back and reflect, we see how we got into these situations.

Each of us has a role to play in this world, and our past experiences prepare us for this moment. The choice I have is whether or not to use these past experiences, skills, and adaptations to prepare for the present.

When I look at these stars, I see the past. The light emitted by their suns comes to us from thousands or millions of years ago. Each has a particular place and a particular reason for being in our Earthly sky. Though they rotate based on the season, the stars don't change. For centuries we used them as guides, long before GPS technology made finding our location as easy as looking at a phone. In that way, the Great Hand is steady, moving us forward from birth to death.

It is tremendously satisfying to know that my place is right here in the present.

NOTE #7

TAKE A BREAK

I love doing electrical work. I like the fascination of putting one wire to the next, twisting them with wire connectors, running cables, and suddenly creating new light.

Many years ago, I was asked to add a light switch to a large rectangular room. There was already one in the front; one just had to be added in the back. I planned it out, figured out what kind of switch to get. (It's called a three-way switch – don't ask me why; it should be called a two way, but two switches = three-way switch, or, in algebraic terms, *switch label=x switches+1.*)

The installation seemed easy enough. First, add a new wire, called the traveling wire. This involved removing the old switch, placing a new wire into the box, and running that wire to the other box through the ceiling to the other side of the room. From the other box, run another set of wires to the lights, and connect the traveling wire.

In the days before YouTube, the internet was still helpful in instructing a novice like me how to do this. However, pulling new wires through the wall was not easy. I pushed, pulled, struggled, used coat hangers, magnets, and anything else so I didn't have to cut the walls. I prayed. I cursed, screamed, and cried, all to no success.

In the end, the project was done, but not without serious damage to my mental state. I knew people would congratulate me on a job well done. They would be impressed.

Sadly, no one noticed.

What would have happened if I had taken my time, instead of trying to do it all in one day? Could I have kept the lights on while I ran new cables? Probably. Would the result have been the same? Definitely.

My stepdad and I used to work on home projects together when I lived nearby. As a master electrician, he knew perfectly well how to fish wire through walls and even create circuits with varying voltages for high-tech companies. One day, while over at my parents' house, my mom said that the telephone had gone out. After talking with AT&T, they determined that a wire had been severed inside the house.

So, we got to work to avoid the cost of hiring a technician. We started up in the attic, looked at the telephone station wire and started reconnecting.

It was the middle of the summer in an attic in Texas. Typically, a home attic in the summer can be as hot as a car, about 120-130°F. We tested each wire slowly, first with one terminal, then another, and another. After a little while of focusing intently on these wires, my stepdad called out:

"Union Break!"

I couldn't believe it! We needed to stop. We were getting close to finding the problem!

"It'll wait a few minutes."

Unlike me, he knew that the fastest way through each problem may not necessarily be the best. After some work time, he knew the importance to stop, to wait, and then resume, with a newly refreshed perspective.

A 2018 article in *Forbes* magazine says that nearly 90% of American workers believe that taking breaks – like a lunch break, or even just a small break – helps them feel refreshed. Focus, creativity, well-being, and self-care are all cited as benefits of regular breaks. Though the article goes on to list ways employers can encourage this behavior, it starts with the personal decision to not continue pushing forward without pausing to recharge.

Washroom and napkin accessory company Tork also produced a study in 2018 regarding workplace happiness and the lunch break. In it, they found that 34% of bosses considered how long an employee took a lunch break in their performance review. They also found that 22% of bosses found that employees who took lunch breaks were less hard working, and that 13% of North American workers think they would be judged negatively if they took lunch breaks. This recent trend has had longer-lasting repercussions – workers are more stressed and more burnt out, breaks, if any, are ignored, and workers are required to punch out and take their lunch breaks on their own time.

When I was unemployed, I worked with a house flipper, helping to install cabinetry, tile, pipe, electrical, or anything else to prepare former run-down homes to receive new occupants. Every day, at precisely 10AM, 12PM and 2PM, we left the (usually hot) job site to go to the local gas station or restaurant for what we affectionately called "teatime." In addition to helping get to know my coworker, it renewed me for more work in the Texas heat and humidity. Though I no longer work in those conditions, the need to connect with other workers during a pause can be even more necessary in an office situation, where often people remain isolated for large portions of the day.

My father used to say to his co-workers, "Give it a rest, it'll still be there tomorrow." Well-liked on every job, Dad knew that near the end of the day no one is

going to notice if the work was done quickly or slowly
if it's eventually done.

NOTE #8

STICK TO THE PLAN

"This or this?"

My sister would use those words as part of a little game when we were children. This one involved choosing the correct hand to receive an intangible, invisible prize. She would hold out her hands, closed into fists, and ask, "This or this?"

I would respond by pointing to one of her hands, saying, "This."

The result was either a buzzer sound, or a ding sound. After guessing correctly – or at least correctly now – the game would switch, and my sister would guess the correct hand, while I held my hands.

Two choices are simple: there's not a lot of room for second-guessing. Many choices? That's another story.

Many nights for dinner we go through this routine. What do you want? Chinese takeout? Italian Takeout?

Salad? Meatless burgers? Honestly, none of it really mattered, so sometimes I'd just pick one to stop the guessing game.

Too many choices are difficult, and it's easy to become overloaded with decisions. Think about it: even a benign question like "Where do you want to go on vacation?"

- Skiing
- Swimming
- Biking
- Driving
- Visiting relatives
- Something new (and hopefully exciting)

We think we deserve lots of choices, but in the end, it can overwhelm. As a result, it's easier to shut down and not want to do anything.

This seems counterintuitive; shouldn't more choices be better? Barry Schwartz disagrees in his book *The Paradox of Choice*. "We end up less satisfied with the result of the choice than we would be if we had fewer options to choose from," he admits. We get overwhelmed because there *might* have been the perfect choice, and we chose the wrong one.

To combat large number of choices, we search out recommendations from the internet. Dozens of people leave reviews. Some are good, but as human beings, we don't fish out the good recommendations, we go for the bad ones! Find the one-star review and instantly that suggestion is planted. For instance:

> *Maybe the service at that restaurant isn't quite as nice as the one across the street.*

> *Would I look better in a pair of jeans from a different company?*

> *What shows should I watch?*

The same is true with daily routines. Do I want to organize my files, clean my desk, rehearse, choose a new piece of music, or stay home and put away clothes? At some earlier time of the day, I may have decided what I want to do, and in what order.

Usually I rate things by priority – my desk is too messy, my clothes are in the dryer. These items need to be addressed first before the rest of the chores, activities or responsibilities can be adjusted.

Then a little time-wasting device happens – I second-guess what I need to be doing. The order of the day needs to be revisited. Sometimes someone contacts me from work, or an email has come in that I must deal with right away.

When I interrupt my plans, for good reason or not, I throw the decisions I made into chaos. I get lost, and indecision takes over. Do I want to continue writing now? Shouldn't I be working on a project in the garage instead? What about the yard?

My office holds the greatest chasms of indecision. I make my way in, thinking there is just one item that needs to be addressed, like preparing the weekly *Choir Notes*. Instead, I wind up having long meetings about chair fabrics, paint, gaps in steps, or other construction related tasks. I wind up looking to make sure the air conditioners are still working. I replace light bulbs or ballasts, knowing I don't want to see some of the volunteers on ladders. At the end, the newsletter is still not done, the music is not picked, and the desk is still messy, because I allowed myself too many distractions. I don't even remember why I came to the church!

So, I came up with a little rule: stick to the plan. I must take care of the problems I have already planned out before I tackle any new ones.

NOTE #9

ALLOW OTHERS TO DO THEIR JOB

Have you had to call in for stuff – especially medical calls or bills requiring a 1-800 number? You call in, sitting at the computer, ready to do other things while waiting on hold. Meanwhile maybe you answer emails or read or throw a tennis ball against the wall. Finally, you get another menu, telling you that "their options have recently changed," and your hold time is still a million minutes.

Finally, you get someone, a real, living person, who tells you that you can order the medical supply you need! Relief and pride swell up as the telephone journey is nearly complete, until you mention the name of your insurance company.

The real, living person's voice breaks in disappointment. We don't work with that company.

Call company B at 1-877-YOU-WAIT. When you call them, they'll be happy to help you, but first listen to the phone for twenty minutes of music interrupted by voices telling you that "their menu options have recently changed." "If this is a medical emergency," they warn you, "hang up and dial 9-1-1."

They then would like to offer a short survey at the end of the call. *No thanks,* you think. It's after 4PM, and I have two more "recently changed" menu options to sort through and reminders to "call 9-1-1 if it's a medical emergency" before they all go home.

Next, they remind you that they are working from home because of the coronavirus, so please expect longer hold times. *Yes,* you mentally respond to their query, *I've tried the website.* That's why I'm calling!

You slowly make your way through the maze that is their phone tree, hoping it isn't messed up by the wrong response. The minutes tick by, and now 5 PM has struck.

Looks like no success today.

In the meantime, you are grateful that God never, ever puts us on hold.

One night at about 2 AM I was again wakened by the newest device I have stuck to my body: a continuous glucose monitor. I moved my insulin pump closer and tried to fall back to sleep. But after the third try, no such luck. I padded down the hall to the closet with the supplies, inserted the last sensor I had, ever aware that tomorrow I needed to make a long drive out of town and would not be able to get more supplies for quite a while.

After the third try at resetting and replacing the sensor, I gave up. I went into the front room with my phone. Teddy, the Pyrenees was asleep on the floor and opened his huge eyes in dismay as I came into his domain at the absolute wrong hour.

I sat down in the chair and called 1-800-something or other. Even at 2AM, the menu options had changed, the wait times were longer-than-expected, and the friendly voice urged me to look at the website first before wasting their precious time calling.

A friendly, live, human being asked for my address, my birthday, my phone number, my email, and finally asked what the problem was. She said she'd send out a new transmitter and sensors, and that I shouldn't worry; they'd arrive in a few days, and in the meantime, go back to taking my blood sugars the old-fashioned way.

"I'm sorry," she began. "Because of COVID, we're taking longer to ship items out to you. It'll be a few days." I told her I was headed to West Texas in the morning, and all she could do was an over-the-phone shrug. After all, it was the middle of the night, and she wasn't in charge of shipping.

At this point, I have two options:

1. Get angry, hurl personal insults to frighten her into speeding up the process of getting me a new set of equipment quickly.
2. Tell her thank you, to have a nice evening, and try to go back to bed, consoled in the fact that there is nothing I can do to change this now.

I chose #2 for two reasons. First, honey really does go farther than vinegar, even in the middle of the night, and maybe if I were nice, she'd make sure the order went into her computer right away. Second, she's just a lady working the night shift, probably from home, who isn't in charge. She doesn't have the Master Computer for my health insurance, the shipping data for the company, or the power to force workers to move faster so I can get what I want.

She's just a person earning an hourly wage on call, trying to do her best, just like the rest of us. I wished her a pleasant evening, and she assured me that the device would be at my doorstep when I got back. What more can I ask?

There are over three million Americans working in call centers, and millions more around the world; many of whom answer calls placed from North America. During the pandemic, many of them are either working from home or at reduced capacity, making wait times even longer. Some websites openly write that wait times may take hours. When my spouse filed for unemployment, he and I sat across the table from one another calling the Texas Workforce Commission in a fervor reminiscent of a radio station concert-ticket-call-in from the 1980's. Each of us received busy signals and hit the redial button over, and over, and over.

When I was in my twenties and going through the doctoral program, I served my time in one of these call centers. One summer I didn't have any teaching responsibilities and needed to earn a living, so I was hired by a credit card company as a call center employee three floors above my dad.

On that upper floor, I answered letters from people who asked why they were on advertising lists, why they had to pay interest this month, and when their bill would arrive. Each day I was also regularly berated via letter by total strangers. My intelligence and lineage were questioned, my love of greed proclaimed, and my silly policies rebuked.

In truth, I was just a guy at a computer studying for his doctoral comprehensive exams. I represented this company about as well or as enthusiastically as my dog represents the food he eats. If I could fix it, I put in the codes and took them off mailing lists or fixed their addresses as needed. I sent payments to the other floor and sent back automated responses generated by the code in the computer. It wasn't the most exciting job, but I needed the work, and I got to spend some time with my dad and see his workplace persona, which oddly enough reminded me of my own.

When it comes to the phone trees and calling the 800 numbers, I hate it. I loathe having to navigate them. I wonder out loud why we can't have someone that answers the phone and puts you on hold in the right area. I watch the minutes tick by and know that it's ultimately wasting my time that I could be spending doing something more meaningful and valuable.

It's not the person's fault that the company saved a buck by installing a phone tree; they just must live with the angry people who get tossed around by it. Like me, they are working; they didn't design the system, and simply must live in its parameters. Like me, that person on the other end of the phone is just doing their job, too.

NOTE #10

SAY THANKS AS OFTEN AS POSSIBLE

When reading about a violinist who appreciated the conductor who moved his gaze, cuing different members of each section. This story resonated with me; I wanted to make sure that as a conductor, I looked at everyone – not just the first chairs. Choirs, being in rows usually by height have a much easier time.

Most singers tell me they prefer if I *don't* look at them, because they think I'm judging their individual voices, but I also know they are much more focused if they feel like I'm watching. Also, fun fact, the easiest way to tell if a chorister knows their part is if the words on their mouth match what's on the page.

At the end of every rehearsal, I say, "Thank you for a great rehearsal." As a chorister, the rehearsals I remember most fondly ended with a "thank you." It meant my time and effort were appreciated, and I want my choristers to feel the same way.

These acknowledgements also connect me to the memory of one of my favorite professors, Dr. Whitlock. She was kind, firm, and extremely knowledgeable about many things – including motivating people to learn. When we finished a lesson or when we all failed part of an exam, she would thank us before sending us out into the wilderness of college.

On the last day of her life, I had the privilege of picking her up from home, as she could no longer drive. She wore an oxygen cannula, and as she slowly shuffled to the car, I worried about her strength to make it up the stairs into the building. I double parked and carried her oxygen canister behind her as we climbed the six grey steps very, very slowly.

"I couldn't *not* be here," she began that last lesson, "because we needed to go over the exam again." She re-taught the material that we had failed. After going through the worksheet, she told us that she was proud of us; that each of us would be great teachers. And she said thanks. Then she ended the class early and I drove her home.

Dr. Whitlock died the next day after fighting breast cancer for many years. Of all the teachers I had in my life, her mark remains the most profound. I do my work as a thanks to the time and energy she and other teachers like her poured into my stubborn head to try and mold me into the best choir director I could be.

That professor taught my class to be grateful for what we received, even if it wasn't passable, like our last exams. Whether things work out well or not, it is best to offer up thanks, to put gratitude out into the universe first, because that energy always comes back.

So far, rehearsals and teaching lessons make for good "thank you" opportunities, but what about others? Here are some examples:

1. *When someone shares a personal story.*

I always realized personal reflections require a level of trust, but never once thought to say thanks! Often, the person sharing is doing so to give themselves clarity and reassurance. A simple thanks goes a long way.

2. *When running late.*

This was another one that surprised me. Lateness usually creates an imposition on the other person or group having to wait, so a simple thanks for waiting can alleviate any resentment.

3. *When receiving unwelcome or unsolicited feedback.*

For those that are saints reading this, it's easy, but for me, hearing someone say something like "you're eating too much mayonnaise," or "can't you cue the sopranos a little better?" can sometimes feel like it's demeaning or belittling. Though a thank you can seem genuine, the intention is to get the "helpful" commenter to leave me alone.

4. *When something exceptional is done.*

This one is a no-brainer, but it needs to be said. Thank people who go above and beyond. The other day we were inspecting the newly painted handrails in the performance center. For the past 20 years, they gleamed a glossy brown and had now been overpainted a stunning, satin black. Combined with the new carpeting, the stairwells gave off a professional, elegant look. It also meant the painter had very carefully put small paintbrushes in every nook and cranny – especially right next to the brand-new carpet – to give that elegant look. Though it was his job, of course he needed a thanks!

Saying thanks is a reminder that we do not exist in a vacuum. When the choir comes to rehearsal and does well or not, when the worker shows up to my house, when the cashier scans my groceries, or when someone makes dinner, say thanks. Someone took their time, energy and effort, and the results are always positive.

NOTE #11

DON'T CREATE A SORRY LETTER

Dear_____,

I'm sorry that I am having to
_____ (insert
function about to do). It would be better if
you'd asked _____
(insert famous person's name) to take care of
_____. In fact,
I have no business doing
_____ and clearly you
should have chosen someone else.

But, since I'm doing it, I'll just suck it up
and do my best; I'll be waiting for your
_____ (text/email) where you tell

*me in all caps "WHAT WERE YOU
THINKING. You are the most horrible
_____ ever."*

*So, I'll be bracing for your horrible
comments.*

Sincerely (or not) and yet regretfully yours,

Me.

One afternoon as I was getting ready to play the piano for a wedding, and this fear reared its ugly head. I imagined, while driving to the wedding venue, writing a sorry letter, a product of ego-driven, silly fear.

As I do things outside my comfort zone, like make videos, play an instrument, or write, I tend to self-sabotage. Though many say mantras like "water off a duck's back," the self-sabotage still exists. It's funny, and I try not to listen to it.

The rational part of my mind says,

> *You're doing great! If you make an error,
> no one will know. After all, how many*

> *people ever written bad responses? You*
> *haven't seen anyone else volunteering to do*
> *the task.*

But the irrational part of my mind is much scarier:

Don't open your email.

Logic and reason win the argument. I march through the problem, and at the end of the day wonder why it seemed so daunting to begin with.

A long time ago, someone gave me a pamphlet called "Partnership," by Vincent P. Collins, and the description reads "This pocket-sized pamphlet is filled with simple, direct advice for anyone with feelings of inadequacy and discouragement." At that point in my life, I was feeling discouraged and inadequate. It said to ask God for help through the day, especially when it came to whatever I was most concerned about when I woke up that morning. My job was to do the part that I could, and God would do the rest.

The feelings of inadequacy didn't go away yet. But I tried it. A few days later, I was given a CD of nun talking about a major change in her life, and in it, she talked about praying to God for the willingness to change everything about her. She uttered only the word "willingness" over and over, as she went about her day.

In those days I drove about an hour to work, so I tried it. I prayed in the morning. I prayed in the car. When I was angry at my job, I prayed there too. The next thing I knew, Monday morning had suddenly morphed into Wednesday. I didn't want to quit the job just yet. In fact, I held on, and it got better. Life got better. The partnership worked.

I like to think of my fear as "the lizard." It runs on instinct only. It makes sure I'm protected, safe, and always comforted. "The lizard" doesn't want my feelings to get hurt or my ego to be bruised. It usually reacts instead of being thoughtful.

"The lizard" is dominated by fear, hunger, and self-preservation. It means well, in that instincts can be a powerful ally. After all, if a tornado is headed toward my house or a Dodge minivan is careening toward my driver side door, fear can remind me what to do. When fear goes out of control and begins making up situations to help "keep me safe," then I have begun to sabotage my helpfulness. This is my ego. It judges my abilities when it has no right. It interprets people's smirk or lack of communication as negative. My ego shows itself as my favorite superpower – mind-reading.

I make fun of myself for doing this now, so that I can be constantly aware of the dangers of listening to "the lizard" part of my brain. The letter at the top of the chapter? That's not me; that's the lizard.

NOTE #12

ALLOW FAILURE AS AN OPTION

O ne of my favorite pieces is Maurice Ravel's (1875-1937) String Quartet in F Major, specifically, the second movement.

Ravel finished this piece in the spring of 1903 when he was 28, and dedicated it to his composition teacher, Gabriel Fauré (1845-1924). (This is the same Fauré who wrote the beloved *Requiem*, *Pavane*, and *Pelléas et Mélisande*.)

At the premiere in 1904, his mentor Fauré was less than impressed. The music review magazine *Musical Times* called it "chiefly remarkable for vagueness of significance, incoherence, and weird harmonic eccentricities."

In effect, it was a dud.

His former teachers at the Paris Conservatory believed Ravel had "no chance, on account of the awful inaccuracies in writing" and he was repeatedly rejected by the judges of the *Prix de Rome* composition award for being, "without any great musicality, a poor, beggarly writer," according to one critic.

Yet Ravel stuck to his work. He orchestrated his *Pavane for a Dead Princess* in 1910, making it extremely popular. Yet, even with these successes, his quartet's fame remained doubtful. Eventually the best critical acclaim was, "When you have heard Maurice Ravel's Quartet in F, you are not very surprised that the gang of pedants at the Institute would not give the *Prix de Rome* to this young artist."

Ravel didn't give up. It's his only string quartet, and the composer would go on to write some incredibly famous pieces; multiple successful piano concertos including one for the left hand, the *Mother Goose Suite*, and the ballet *Daphnis and Chloé*. By the time of his death, Ravel had achieved some fame as a composer.

After his death, his most noted works were his orchestral arrangement of Modest Mussorgsky's *Pictures at an Exhibition,* and *Bolero*, a Spanish dance tune with a single, repeating theme that slowly changes over 15 minutes. Music texts today consider him a French impressionist along with one of his musical heroes, Claude Debussy.

Though the quartet suffered in its early reception, today it's widely regarded as one of the most popular in chamber music repertoire. Eventually, the work was performed in London, then Berlin, and spread through Europe, performed often enough to compare different renditions by different groups.

How often do we create something that appears to be broken and unsuccessful, only for it later to have a life of its own? In 1904 after the quartet's cold reception in Paris, Ravel could have taken the manuscript, put in a fire, and burned it. He could have gone back to driving trucks like he did during World War I, but Ravel continued composing. He studied jazz with George Gershwin, and he kept writing music.

Ravel's tenacity became the bedrock of his success as a composer, and though his works aren't as prolific as Schubert or Beethoven, he nonetheless made a great impression on music that still resonates today.

How often do we arrive at a moment in our careers only to walk away with a failure? We watch movies where the tag line is "failure is not an option." The music swells, and we think, *yeah, they're going to do this!* In the movies, "they" always do.

The real world isn't always like the movies.

One of the problems in professional literature is how we are guaranteed success by trying tips outlined in some new article, written by someone who seems to have no failures and a terrific bio. People tell us even in a chosen field, that we're bad. We can't pass muster or never become scholars or teachers or tradesmen or mechanics. Ravel's lesson is clear: if we have the determination, we prove them wrong.

So, we fail. So what? Did we learn from the failure? Can we keep going and try again?

God has three answers to our prayers, when it comes to requests and avoiding failure:

Yes.

Not yet.

or:

I've got something better.

The aloof, logical Ravel had something better waiting for him. Usually, so do we.

NOTE #13

STAY AWAY FROM INTELLECTUAL VICES

The first day of class always excited me. I walked into the classroom, having taught this music history overview many times. This was day one – syllabus day. I explained how we would be learning about some of the major composers from the 16th through 20th centuries who were influential in western music.

I was really surprised when a woman near the back blurted out, "Who decided that these are the composers we should study?" Up until then, I had never thought Bach, Beethoven, Chopin, or Schubert as controversial.

"These are the ones whose works survived," I explained. "These composers left a considerably broad mark on western music history. Some of these composers were revered and imitated. Some were just liked because they were prodigies. Some were loved for their technical skill at their instrument. All stood the test of time."

"So, you just read it out of some book," she challenged. "Our textbook just came up with these and that's what you're going to teach."

I tried to explain that it wasn't just this textbook; I used several books for teaching this class. This was a taste of the wonderful world of art music that influences what we hear today.

As a music researcher, I often asked questions – why was this instrument the preferred accompaniment? Why did we use this type of ornament in the 17th versus 18th centuries?

This was something else, though, like a challenge to the course – a course that she chose to take. Though the dialogue was interesting, I needed to move on, because I couldn't spend another 20 minutes discussing rationalizations for teaching western music canon in a course whose description was, "discuss the canon of Western historical music and its influence on society."

She dropped the class. I wasn't sorry to see her go.

I try to reach every student where they are. Some need extra confidence. Some need more data and analysis. Some require extra explanations.

This student needed none of those things. She was interested in her own idea that she didn't need to be here. The premise of my class was that we use music everywhere today for both enjoyment and enhancement. In short, understanding music history helped awareness of its powerful manipulation in our society.

Sometimes people debate an issue. They present their side, and sometimes I'm wrong. This person only cared about her own opinion, and as far as music went, she was closed to anything else.

"Contempt prior to investigation," William Paley calls this. He was a late eighteenth-century philosopher and clergyman who wrote *View of the Evidences of Christianity*.

"[It] is an intellectual vice," he writes, "from which the greatest faculties of mind are not free."

We must be careful that our beliefs can withstand debate and challenge, or they become an echo chamber. This is especially true when I turn the echo chamber inward on myself, and it becomes a delicious, ego-driven trap.

"Contempt prior to investigation" isn't just objecting to the canon of western music; it's the opinions and ideas we ferment about ourselves in a twisted fashion. No person, place or idea has ever destroyed my soul as much as my own ego. Refusing other people's ideas, I convince myself that my negative opinion is paramount; that other people's opinions don't matter.

How does one overcome an intellectual vice?   Here are some of the common ones.

1. Tell on yourself.

This is the best time to tattle. When I'm insecure, emotional, and afraid, I find a friend, co-worker, family member, or whomever, and tell them. I explain why I feel this way. When I have done this, I find that the reason I feel small usually seems somewhat ridiculous when I share it outside my own head. Remember, there is more fear in darkness.

2. Review your history.

Have you done something like this before? Has it always been unsuccessful? If so, can you put it behind you?

I remember the first time I traveled overseas. I was alone on a flight to Germany, headed to Romania to conduct an orchestra. As the door closed, I thought *What have I done?* I had prepared for months for the musical part of the journey, and had obsessed over maps, language, and travel blogs. Still, I was terrified. What if everyone laughs at my conducting? More importantly, what if I can't find my hotel?

Then I remembered how often I had traveled alone to other cities. I knew where to go. And yes, at the end of the day, I did get lost, but it wasn't that bad. My history prepared me for this mission.

3. *Know your mission.*

My mission, in my previous example – conducting the orchestra – was much bigger than my fear of traveling overseas. When I prepare for a new concert, conduct a new ensemble, go into a new situation, I keep my eyes on the *mission.*

Our ultimate mission is *to be of service to others.* Whether that means I conduct, sing, play the piano, run electrical wiring, or rake the yard, I am making a difference. Fear tells me that I am alone. Faith tells me that I am part of a larger whole; my job and my actions relate to others, and they support me.

4. *Connect with others who will help.*

When I applied for my current job, one of my long-time friends, Yung-Chiu, invited me over to her house. She and her husband, a piano-playing power couple, walked with me through the pieces that I would be conducting in an audition the next day. In return, my friend Debbie, my husband, and I practiced online interviews with her.

Yung-Chiu is one of the friends that helps me walk through my career and my life. We read each other's writing and listen to each other's concerts. We encourage one another, and root for one another. At the end of the day, our friends want us to succeed.

An intellectual vice like stubbornness shuts us down. In that student's case, she was separated from the knowledge and fun in that class. In my case, I'm separated from the opportunity to be useful.

How do we overcome "contempt prior to investigation?"

Investigate!

NOTE #14

LOVE YOUR FRIENDS

L amenting the loss of my friend Mike (not his real name), I had a long conversation with Tiana, who introduced me to this poem:

People always come into your life for a
reason, a season, or a lifetime.
When you figure out which it is, you know
exactly what to do.

When someone is in your life for a
REASON, it is usually to meet a need you
have expressed outwardly or inwardly.

They have come to assist you through a
difficulty,
Or to provide you with guidance and
support,

To aid you physically, emotionally, or even spiritually.

They may seem like a Godsend to you, and they are.
They are there for the reason you need them to be.
Then, without any wrongdoing on your part or at an inconvenient time,
This person will say or do something to bring the relationship to an end.

Sometimes they die. Sometimes they just walk away.
Sometimes they act up and force you to take a stand.
What we must realize is that our need has been met, our desire fulfilled; their work is done.
The prayer you sent up has been answered and it is now time to move on.

When people come into your life for a SEASON,
It is because your turn has come to share, grow, or learn.
They may bring you an experience of peace or make you laugh.

Singing in the Moment

*They may teach you something you have
never done.*

*They usually give you an unbelievable
amount of joy.
Believe it! It is real! But, only for a season.
And like Spring turns to Summer and
Summer to Fall,
The season eventually ends.*

*LIFETIME relationships teach you lifetime
lessons;
Those things you must build upon in order
to have a solid emotional foundation.
Your job is to accept the lesson, love the
person anyway;
And put what you have learned to use in all
other relationships and areas in your life.*

*It is said that love is blind but friendship is
clairvoyant.
Thank you for being part of my life,
Whether you were a reason, a season or a
lifetime.*

-Anonymous

When I released Mike's friendship, I was devastated.
Mike listened while I was moving to my current home.

During the months I struggled to complete the purchase of my house, he would talk of his own problems, and they didn't seem as scary or as difficult.

I would realize in retrospect Mike never lifted a box, or a finger. It was a one-sided friendship. As our paths began to diverge, our values and ideas didn't seem to align any more.

Carla, another friend I met living out of state, spent a lot of time with me when I first moved there. We were in the same field, ate together regularly, and even vacationed together.

After I moved back to Texas, our conversations grew shorter and less frequent. That friendship remains a shadow of its former self. Without drama, it has faded.

Today, surrounded by many wonderful people, my gratitude grows when I hear from my friends. There are only so many hours in a day, and only so many friends that one can be close to. Time is our one resource that can never be replenished or reused. It is, of all the gifts, the most special gift we can give to our friends.

In 2005, the Australian Longitudinal Study of Aging found that people with more friends tended to live 22 percent longer. Of course, friends take a long time to cultivate. We may have one or two "best" friends, some others with whom we interact with frequently, and a much larger group of people we are friendly with. Among many authors, the idea of "friends" never means "Facebook friends." In fact, Dr. Saul Levine wrote in *Psychology Today*:

> *Some of these online friendships are more 'virtual' than real.*

Who are our close friends? How do we know? Those that are closest are the ones that we hear from and talk to regularly. They are in our inner circle.

When I first met Nancy, she was surly, tough, and rather unrefined. But there was something about her that caught my attention. She loved her family. She was extremely proud of her daughter, son-in-law, and especially her grandchildren.

Nancy and I first met on Sunday mornings eating breakfast together. She cared for her mom, babysat two grandkids, and genuinely tried to help her family.

Nancy had no formal education but had a great deal of real-world experience, which I desperately needed. I talked to her about God. She talked to me about how to navigate untrustworthy people. We traveled to conferences together and listened to people talk about spirituality and how to pray.

After I moved back to Texas, I talked to Nancy faithfully every week. Usually, she told me how her grandkids had grown, or how proud she was of her kid. I shared with her about my new jobs. We laughed a lot, and my new life was bearable.

The day that Nancy passed away, her son-in-law called me from her phone. I answered in the grocery store parking lot and was stunned to hear that my closest friend was gone. I still hear her in my head, usually after I made some bad decision. Her advice is right there, along with her voice.

My sister Heather is my closest lifetime friend. She has seen me through the ups and downs of schooling, through good jobs and bad jobs, and through the tumultuous years of growing up. When I was working on my dissertation, when she encountered a difficult class, when I wrote books and articles, we were there for one another. When I moved back to Texas, unsure of my next career, my sister was there.

How can we tell who is a friend? Friends give one thing – their time. They see opportunities to get together and invite one another to do so. They talk on the phone and listen to one another. They respect our choices and voice their concerns. Friends give of themselves and miss us when we're absent. They expect nothing from us, and we expect nothing from them, yet both continue to give freely. After all, being a friend is how to remain one.

Sometimes, we must let friends go. Occasionally they disagree with us, but feeling repeatedly belittled or jilted, or feeling used may indicate it's time to reconsider that friendship. If I'm putting in more work, or if it seems one-sided, it may be time to let them go. In the end, I can do it with love and respect, remembering the good times we shared.

NOTE #15

REMEMBER WE ARE ALL ALIENS

As a college professor, I fit in about as well as a pig at the ballet. My colleagues would discuss learning outcomes and politics at the lunch table. I was more interested in knowing why the duct work made silly noises. Eventually, I met other people like me – great teachers who didn't fit and marveled at the strange politics of postsecondary schools.

One year I was assigned to the assessment committee, which our school was sadly lacking. We had a dean who yelled at us that we weren't ready for the next accreditation visit. He regularly turned red in the face and stormed out of the meetings, and yet we never accomplished anything. My friend Steven (not his real name), possessing enough real-world experience not to worry about the boss's tantrums, would not take the boss too seriously.

Steven lived in a log cabin in the woods. He obsessed about teaching his students his subject, even though very few of them would major in his area, and he worked hard to make sure his students were as well-prepared as they could be. He didn't fit into the professor-crowd. Together, we were two misfits in an academic dystopia.

Not fitting in is a common theme for a lot of people. It's why postmodern stories tend to involve irony, and why our heroes aren't "good guys" or "bad guys" anymore. Postmodern heroes tend to be awkward, shy, and reserved. They don't get along with everyone at the office. They aren't community leaders and don't have grand social lives.

One of my favorite examples of the post-modern hero is the character from *Star Trek: The Next Generation,* Reginald Barclay.

At first, Mr. Barclay is an annoyance; later he's a hinderance, and eventually, despite his misfitted persona, he becomes a hero. We, the audience, start to identify with Barclay. We understand his fear of others, and his retreat into a fantasy world. We see his brilliant mind at work, solving problems that perplex others. Mr. Barclay is a hero because he thinks in his own way.

In short, Mr. Barclay is a character.

My friend Lauren calls this an "introvert." I never took the Meyers-Briggs test to see where I fall, but I realize, I too am like her, an introvert. Though we used to talk at length in the mornings before work, we rarely enjoyed crowds. Despite our seeming awkwardness in social situations, yet both of us are musical performers who love the stage. How does that work?

Lauren described introverts as "people that gain their energy from within. Extroverts gain their energy from outside."

Megan Malone of *introvertdear.com* writes, "As introverts, we spend a lot of time in our inner worlds. Because of this, many of us are incredibly self-aware."

I spent many years wondering, when in group situations, why I was more comfortable washing the dishes, standing outside talking to only one other person, or refusing to attend social functions. I thought there may have been something wrong. At the same time, I loved teaching in front of large groups. I give talks and sermons – certainly "introverts" don't do that! If I were quick-witted enough or funny, I would be a stand-up comic. Yet I can travel, eat, and vacation alone. I love to spend hours in diners reading murder mystery novels instead of having grand conversations. My time in the fellowship hall of the church is minimal because there are so many discussions happening all at once that I feel overwhelmed.

I work best in crowds when I have a job to do. Though not shy, I too feel "alien," and make do in a world that seems to be full of extroverts. I love rehearsing, but once the rehearsal is over or the concert finished, I love to focus on the next project, or put all the "stuff" away, so that I can contemplate the last hour and how to make the next one better.

If I feel like I have a job to do, I embrace the awkwardness. It's nice to fit in, but it's also nice to remain in the background.

We all need to exist in the current moment. After all, being an alien means we are not just different, but memorable.

NOTE #16

OPEN THE WINDOW

My college choir director used to shout, "OPEN THE WINDOW!!! If you listen carefully enough, you can hear the other choir yelling out another anthem!!!"

It was a metaphor to listen for the ridiculous, for the unimaginable and ludicrous. It meant to do something unexpected to get better results. For me, it meant traveling to a different place, closing myself off, and writing.

Typically, I travel alone, since someone has to stay behind to watch the dogs. My husband takes his own trips, too, and occasionally we vacation together. Recently, my favorite vacations involved somewhere to write, somewhere to drive, somewhere to walk, and somewhere to reflect.

I never pictured myself as a writer – but I do enjoy teaching and I love communicating with people. So, when I committed to weekly letters to the choir five years ago, I was surprised at how much I genuinely enjoyed writing each week. Sometimes I received comments back. Sometimes I just marveled at the words.

A few years ago, I felt a need, like a flower in a field of concrete, to write some of the lessons I'd learned. I wanted to help others, and, after 15 years since pounding out a dissertation, I felt like it was time to contribute, first to the choral music community, then, more importantly, to the friends, congregation members, and colleagues whom I spent time with and worked with.

I wanted to open the window.

As a graduate student, I befriended a professor who was a prolific writer. At regular intervals, he left town, taking writing retreats. When I was 25 years old, that sounded intensely boring; I wanted to be in the middle of big cities, ensembles, concerts, and activity. I didn't want to just sit and write.

As I seasoned, the idea of occasionally divesting my responsibilities and writing appealed to me, but I still wasn't ready.

Then one day something happened. I had given a workshop on conducting, and Mary, one of my handbell choir members exclaimed, "You should write this stuff down!"

Weeks later I mulled this comment, and realized that if I didn't start now, I never would. I wrote during my spare time but kept getting interrupted by life. I would get parts written, only to abandon them for weeks or months at a time.

Finally, I decided to try what my professor did – I brought my books, my food, my coffee, and my old laptop, and found a place to go.

I rented a house, staying for a cold week in January, and renewed my writing in earnest. I wrote several hours a day; as much as I could in the morning, followed by a walk around noon, and more writing in the evenings.

After a week, the book started to take shape. A few months later, I did it again. I spent more time writing during the day and visiting a friend in the evenings. I continued hammering away at the book I had dreamed about only two years earlier.

I felt guilty leaving my husband behind. Each time I would ask, "Are you sure it's ok?" I discovered he wanted the whole house to himself too.

I gave myself permission to open the window.

Before, I considered myself a "one trick pony," and that trick was directing choirs. Looking at my personality versus a "writer's persona," I saw a huge chasm. Writers are alone. They are intellectual. They associate with people who use large words. They see the world differently. They pontificate. They enunciate.

I'm none of those things. I'm direct, bold, down-to-earth, snarky, crass, and only somewhat intellectual. I know lots of people. I tell dumb jokes in rehearsal. In short, I'm not the "type" of person who writes. I only write because I want to make sure others learn from my mistakes.

As I continue writing weekly notes to the choir, I realize how much I really enjoy it. The more I write, the more I realized I enjoy it! As a result, I write more.

Why should we open the window?

1. *We are facing a fear.*

Doing new things breaks us free of some of that fear because it leads to success, even if it means performing the same task in a new location.

2. *We learn more about ourselves.*

A few summers ago, I took a storytelling course. The instructor prompted us to tell where we felt "most authentic," and then choose a partner to describe it. I recounted to another participant about rebuilding a wooden fence. I spoke of the wood, the heaviness, the screws, and the sense of accomplishment. As I traded story partners, my story modified, and by the third iteration something new struck. I realized building the fence was something my dad, now long deceased, and I would have done together.

3. We stimulate creativity.

Doing something unusual like riding my bicycle through the unique and wooded paths along the creek as part of my ride home certainly wasn't the most direct route between the church and my house, but it did push me out of my regular routine. It allowed me to see and experience the greenery around me on a hot summer day, the sand beneath the wheels, the way my mind wandered because I was totally alone with my thoughts.

When it came to writing, I opened the window with a crack, and eventually flung it wide open. Who goes on trips by themselves to remote places to write? Who spends hours sitting hunched over a computer deciding if this paragraph makes sense? Who coaxes their friends to read their hefty manuscripts? Who asks loved ones to listen to drafts to see if the overall impact works? Someone who opens the window does.

What ideas have been put on your back burner? Designing a video game? Painting? Studying a language? Playing an instrument? Jumping out of an airplane? Travel? Flying a powered paraglider? Playing wheelchair basketball? Coaching little league? Becoming a volunteer counselor?

Just open the window.

Note #17

Wait for More to be Revealed

Years ago, a new pastor was appointed to my church. He was funny, down-to-earth, loved Texas A&M, and had a deep, resonant voice. He possessed a reverence for liturgy and an engaging sermon delivery. He prayed on his knees and believed in the restorative power of scripture, liturgy, and prayer. He attempted to live by spiritual principles and habits, and his humanness made him identifiable to many.

Imagine my surprise when one day he needed me to substitute for him at the small service.

I was dumbfounded. What would I even say?

I really respected this man. I knew he was strong-willed, like me, and yet was always trying to increase his spiritual connection, like me. He seemed to "get" me; we had similar temperaments and similar speaking styles. He once told me that he learned to preach by watching comedians tell their stories.

To say it was an irony that someone like me would lead a church service was an understatement. In the past I've given talks, lectures, and workshops. I revel in speaking in front of others. I've even talked about God, waxing prophetically. But this man wanted a formal, Sunday-Morning-from-the-pulpit sermon.

God, you have a sense of humor.

I looked up the prescribed readings for that week: the parable of the seeds and the sower. Like preparing for class, I took notes, read what other people said, and wrote my sermon.

Around Wednesday of that week, notes in hand, I paced back and forth between the kitchen and backyard. I hated what I had written. In what I refer to as the "Wednesday Crisis," I rewrote the entire sermon, creating one that sounded more like my voice, complete with jokes, everyday language, and new thoughts and ideas. By the time Sunday morning came around, I was comfortable talking about that parable.

After all the work, the angst, the pacing, the re-writing, and the rehearsing, something amazing happened. It was just another Sunday. The week was over, a new week of work had begun, and, as far as the congregation went, Sunday morning was over, and it was time for lunch on Main Street.

It meant a new experience was available that I hadn't been aware of. It meant doing something new and, despite the fact I might never be excellent at it, I also would not be the worst, and I might enjoy it. The awful terror of writing and delivering a sermon was real and I experienced it firsthand. Next time it would be a little bit easier.

My friend Tomi used to say "more will be revealed" all the time. Everyone she met heard this phrase at one point or another, and usually it had to do with difficult circumstances. She would say those words as a reminder that we only know a little, and that as time goes on, we'd learn and understand more and more.

"More will be revealed" is as much about twenty-twenty hindsight as it is about taking leaps of faith. Years earlier, I sat in front of the phone in my office, deliberating whether I should even call this church to interview. In what turned out to be the start of the next stage of my career, more was revealed.

If not for that pastor having faith in me, my career path would be quite different right now. I just did what I was asked to do, and as a result, my life changed dramatically.

NOTE #18

BE A CHANNEL

The twinkling lights shined through the vase on the altar, and yet the strand between vases was submerged beneath a few pieces of black tape. The idea came to me after driving through the neighborhood. It was Christmas and many houses were decked out with lights, inflatable Santa's, and other decorations.

My husband has a funny way of seeing things and immediately judging them. Once the judging is done, he then mutters, usually under his breath, about the décor, especially if it's not up to his standards.

I think it's hilarious. Most of these things don't really warrant a second thought to me.

In one case, though, it was a set of lights: one wrapped around a tree to the left, and one on the tree to the right. My husband did not object to the tree-wrapping. Instead, it was the line of lights that drooped from one tree, across the ground before snaking up the next. My husband wondered why they left the lights run along the ground.

"Well how would you do it?" I inquired.

"Bury the lights between the trees."

I rolled my eyes, feigning annoyance, but it was just Michael being, well, Michael.

As the senior stylist at a luxury department store here in Houston, Michael is expected to have grand ideas and great vision. He never disappoints in that area, as his displays always use a great deal of thought and inspiration. The best part is that he just seems to magically come up with inspiration.

When the time came to decorate for advent and I needed something new, I brought lights from our attic and stuck them in the little clear vases on the altar.

The conversation with Michael flashed in my head, and I knew there were other designers in the congregation who would judge my little Advent decorations. Out came the tape to hide the lights between vases. Now no one could see unwanted connections.

Inspiration seems to come in these little quiet insights.

In rehearsal inspiration comes like this too. One evening in handbell rehearsal we were having trouble with a set of rhythms that repeated underneath a soaring melody, but the rhythms appeared suddenly, and seemed to elude everyone. We counted. We clapped. Nothing worked. Until the thought crossed my mind, *"why don't you make up a phrase?"*

Earlier that season we hosted a choir contest. The tour company recommended bringing snack food for both the directors and the judges. I chose Dunkin' Donuts, which became the inspiration for the chant:

"Munch-kins are ve-ry tas-ty, munch-kins are ve-ry tas-ty."

I needed a chant to enforce a syncopated rhythm. We found other words to use for the rhythm, including my dogs' names, the word "hand-bells," and many others, but the inspiration came from the donut shop. The players learned the rhythm and they loved the piece.

Sometimes insights happen in extreme situations. Exiting the freeway one evening, I drove down a busy four-lane street, having driven in the dark for more than 45 minutes with little sign of civilization. The streetlights blazed a path well-marked by cars' headlights. Ahead, on the right was a Wal-Mart, with people driving in and out, but that wasn't my destination, so I continued ahead in the other lane.

Suddenly a car pulled out, probably not seeing me. I hit my brakes but knew it wouldn't be enough; I was going to hit the car and wreck my old SUV.

"Aim for the rear bumper," came the thought.

I didn't think. I followed instructions. His rear bumper was hard, cold metal. I focused on it and turned the wheel, crossing into the other lane of traffic as the old explorer slowed.

By the time I stopped, the car had whisked past just barely, and was stopped halfway into the opposing lanes. We had missed each other.

Thanks, I prayed. Heart pounding, I continued to my destination, grateful that I was not injured and my vehicle intact.

When I keep my mind open, these little insights come. Some might say this is my conscience; a voice of rational meta-thought brought about from experience. I choose to believe that this voice emanates from a higher being. I choose to depend on it.

NOTE #19

ACCEPT IT

When I started conducting choirs, I figured that my will could influence and herd others into doing what they were supposed to. Sing this way, make this phrase better, accent here. All it would take is a flick of the wrist, a funny story or an insightful comment.

That didn't work, until I learned the little rule about *internal acceptance.* Conducting became an exercise in acceptance. When rehearsal goes badly, it doesn't mean I'm a horrible conductor or a bad person.

Before this, I was certain that every sub-par rehearsal or performance was my fault. If the choir didn't perform it right the first time, if I couldn't sing the passage perfectly, if I couldn't play it, there was something wrong with me. I failed to realize the word *re*-hearsal has "re" in it; meaning to do again!

I had to accept that things wouldn't be perfect all the time, or even most of the time. Then I had to look and see: what can I change? What can I make better? Do I have an idea that I aspire to, and how can I get it as close to that idea as possible?

As a conductor, I confidently can say that almost nothing is in my control, and I like it that way. Instead of getting frustrated about the way things went, I can ask myself what needs to be changed. Is there a technique or pedagogical tool that I can use to make a passage better? Should the choir stand? Are they focused? Am I focused? If not, what can I do to fix that?

Today I do my best and leave the results up to my God. I am responsible for the process: I show up, I try to explain through gesture and speech what I'm looking for, but ultimately, it's up to the ensemble to do their best.

Sometimes things happen in performance that I didn't anticipate or expect. A soloist gets nauseous and quickly leaves the stage right after his solo. A French horn player misses a note. The ceiling leaks on someone's music because a powerful thunderstorm is roaring outside. The saxophone player drops her mouthpiece hours before the concert, and it shatters. I have no power over these instances.

Sometimes, the performance comes off badly. Once, as a singer in the choir, we performed a spiritual where one section missed an entrance, and the piece was less than successful. The conductor turned to the choir, smiled, acknowledged the applause, and bowed as if it were a triumphant success. Then he turned to the choir, hands out as though directing the applause, and acknowledged us to rousing applause from the hall.

Most of the audience didn't know the difference and didn't care. As an audience member, when I watch students make mistakes, I find myself rooting for them even more. *Come on, you can do it,* I think to myself.

As the one making the music, I can find myself overwhelmed by the errors. When I played piano, I was stuck in judgement mode, instead of enjoying. I thought that the enjoyment came *after* the notes had been perfected; *after* the "real" work had been done. How does one make music sound musical when stuck in the mechanics of making music?

This does not mean I just leave everything up to chance. There is time when good, thorough study of the mechanical parts of music are necessary. What *should* the notes sound like? Should I practice that section slower? Should I try with one hand? Would this be better using different rhythms? Can I count each rhythm? Should I clap or sing the part?

The same can be applied to other fields too. I find choir financial reports a special thrill, especially if I get to make a pie chart showing how we spent money this year. Did everything balance? Did I forget the carry-over from last year at the top of the page?

Never mind that every year I must Google "how to make a pie chart" with spreadsheet software.

This led to a new realization: solving problems is fun. In fact, the more challenging the problem, the more interesting it is. The Hungarian American psychologist Mihaly Csikszentmihalyi refers to this in his work as "flow," the perceived passage of time. In an educational setting, "flow" is created through a balance between difficulty and skill level. In "flow," time seems to pass quickly. When I'm confronted with a challenge, whether it be conducting a concert, creating an accounting report, or finalizing a rehearsal plan, "flow" occurs when I work on something challenging enough to match my skill level.

Today I only have two choices: accept or change. If I can't change it, I must accept it the way it is. When I used to sit outside and wonder how to get my ensemble to sing better, I was regularly perplexed and upset.

Today I look at the problems, and I don't get mad. I break them down, fix them or accept them.

NOTE #20

IGNORE THE FEAR. IT LIES

Planes used to frighten me.

Days before boarding, I started thinking. *How would I react if the plane went down? What would be my final thoughts?* I made plans with my friends to make sure they got this or that if I died. I'd tell them where my apartment key was, who gets my plants, and who to notify.

Sometimes I'd get brave. Occasionally I didn't drink before I got on the plane. I sat in the rear-facing seats. I tried to act unafraid, but still looked at the ground, far below me. The worst was the planning and plotting, each time, before the flight.

Then something happened.

On a trip to New York with my community choir, one of my students was arrested, and I worked with another choir member to get him out. After a series of very strange events – showing up in a courtroom, meeting a random attorney, watching defendant after defendant go by - we got this kid out of jail. Now at this point I had no clue how jails and fines and holding cells worked. We just arrived at the courthouse, hoping that would fix it.

After that event, I realized I couldn't explain everything that had occurred that night. It was a gift – one that I didn't earn and didn't deserve. I was so moved by what happened that weekend that, as we flew back to Austin, the fear had just disappeared.

Many years later, and after flying many more times, I became interested in these large, winged machines. No longer were they instruments of terror, but vessels of opportunity. Yes, there were moments where the plane shook or dived that still were scary, but they were followed by other times: where the plane took off, where it soared through clouds, where the people working on board were chatting with other pilots nearby. I discovered that there is a whole ecosystem of people whose lives and livelihoods were connected to airplanes: the pilots and flight attendants, the booking agents, the rental car associates, the food workers, the credit card servicers, the hotel workers, the ramp agents, the gate agents, the FAA workers, all moving together in concert to get me and my "stuff" from one place to another.

One day I did the craziest thing I could think of – I took a flying lesson. It was my first time in a single-engine propeller plane. I had no idea how any of the controls worked, let alone that there are foot controls! The instructor explained some of the basics to me, and then lined us up for a "touch and go," where we would circle around the little airport, touch the ground, and return to the air. The plane lifted almost magically, and the instructor told me something I have never forgotten:

"Remember, the plane always *wants* to be airborne."

I started to fall in love with flying. I looked forward to feeling the lift of the plane. I loved the way that such a huge machine naturally picks up off the ground. I watched how the people interacted with one another. I reveled in the feel of the seats. I enjoyed the freedom from my cell phone and from the tyranny of the internet. I felt the hush that is only me, the few people around me, and the hum of the engines. I marveled the way the wings change shape to slow us down, or how we valiantly climb through clouds of storms, only to suddenly burst through. My mind developed soundtracks: trumpet melodies as the plane ascends higher; French horns as the aircraft lined up in approach to the runways.

That was it. I was hooked. I got to take the controls for a few minutes, doing circles around our small town, and after coming back down to earth, I felt invincible. After all, if someone like me can fly a plane, those guys with a zillion hours at the controls should be fine – without my input.

I never worry about whether I'll survive the ride anymore. Though there are times that the plane shakes especially hard, or bumps or falls tremendously fast, I know that not only am I protected by the force of lift which comes about thanks to speed, but I am safe and protected in God's hands, too. No matter what happens, I am always in God's hands.

NOTE #21

ACT AS THOUGH YOU ARE

I wanted to be a conductor for as long as I remember. The music making, teamwork, artistry, and the elegance I knew was in my body. I felt the music of symphonies and choirs. I could talk to others. I could make things happen.

I also possessed the grace of an ox.

Seriously, I'm clumsy. I trip all the time. For our wedding, we received 6 glasses. Between washing them and drinking out of them, we're down to three. It's like a constant reminder of my inability to move with grace.

Conductor? Nope. Conductors are suave. They move with elegance. They embody the music, and they live kind-of outside the real world in their own, governed only by the music they embody.

At least, they are supposed to.

When I started with my first church choir, I felt no elegance, no motion. I couldn't run a rehearsal with poise and style. I had great expectations for myself and had no idea how to live up to them. Moving from job to job, the element that seemed to always stand in the way was my own feeling of inadequacy. If they only knew I was a fraud, they wouldn't like anything about me. I kept going to school. I became a professor. It didn't help. The nagging self-doubt remained.

In 2006, I met Maestro Gutter. He was an accomplished conductor, a family man, and a genuine person. He didn't act as though the music was his only drive. He talked about family, his life, and his students. And yet, he conducted and taught with so much love and fire that it finally clicked. He was a fantastic conductor who had a work-life balance that I yearned for and couldn't ever find. He was someone who thoroughly enjoyed his work.

He knew how to fix some of the dreadful mistakes I had inside of me. He saw the heaviness in my posture, the awkward way I held a baton, and my strong desire to use subdivisions in my conducting. He showed me different methods of conducting tempo changes and modeled how I could teach conducting. In short, spending time with this man caused me to re-evaluate my self-view.

I also watched other colleagues do things that only conductors do. They wore their button-up shirts untucked, especially in the unairconditioned concert hall. They spent time smoking cigarettes and drinking coffee while pouring over Tchaikovsky or Wagner or Mozart scores. They laughed about their own problems in their conducting. Together, we learned to survive in a foreign land, where none of us knew the language and all of us needed to communicate.

I came home from that experience with my shirt untucked. I bought a new backpack and a new, round grip baton that I still use. I spent more time at the piano and less with recordings. I watched my back to make sure it wasn't stooped over. I breathed. In time, I became more comfortable face to face with the orchestra.

As I started to feel more like a conductor, I began to act like one. I already had the ensembles, the training, the experience, but I needed the belief.

There are times when it's better to act than to think. First, when it involves other people, like my choir, it's inappropriate for me to deliberate the best course of action on the podium. We'd never get anything done if I polled for opinions at every opportunity.

Second, it's better to act when my thinking is circular, such as when I'm stuck in a resentment or anger. Sometimes movement and action stop a repeating thought cycle.

Third, I act when I need to repeat what I've learned. When I am preparing a choir for a concert, we practice the notes and rhythms, and then we practice what it's like to stand for the entire program. We practice what it's like to walk on stage, how to bow, and all the minor details of performance. I send out rehearsal notes with details about how I'm going to direct sections. I arrange seating charts and give my OK for how the room is set up. This type of "rehearsal" action is so rewarding because it's a mirror of the task, concert, or event I'm preparing.

I'll never be the perfect conductor, but today I am a good one, because I was open, because I learned, and because I watched how some of the "real" conductor's work.

NOTE #22

IT'S NOT WHAT YOU THINK

She looked down as I took my keys and my badge off my neck. I hated wearing those things. Having a badge and being a number has never appealed to me. In fact, during my first year at that school, badges weren't necessary.

I had been fired. Again. Technically, I'd been non-renewed. But I had received in the mail a letter telling me I would not be coming back. I had just moved there two years earlier, bought a house, took back my old church position, and had taken back this job that I had held 15 years earlier. My dog and I walked through the streets of the small town often seeing people we knew. Soon all of that would come to an end.

College professors are acutely aware that they are always replaceable. When faculty approach tenure, we are reminded of this, because we must either have an outstanding level of research, service, scholarship, and teaching skills, or find another job. So, here I was, again, handing over my keys.

One of my bosses often interjected his opinions on running my choir and voice programs. He was dismissive, rude, and he'd scream a lot. My heart would race as we'd go into meetings where he got angry while others would stand by and watch.

The day the non-renewal letter came offered something else – a level of peace. At first my friends were angry and wanted to fight. My students – now former students – were upset and wanted me to stay on. My friends vowed to fight for my job. I appealed the decision half-heartedly. Did I really want to go back there?

No.

After handing over my keys, I changed careers. I moved to a large city for the first time. I started working in a large church, directing a choir yearning for more advanced literature and a boss who never once raised his voice to me.

My friend Tomi used to say revenge is like drinking poison and hoping the other person would die. Years later, I still thought of this man. I wondered when he would get his just reward. I was incredulous that he was promoted instead.

One day I was rereading a book that said, "forgive everyone for everything." I couldn't do that. So, I prayed. I knew I needed to.

"Dear God: I hate that jerk, but if you would, give him the same gifts you have given me."

Every day, I prayed this. Eventually I quit caring about him. It was in the past.

I realized the stupidity of this old resentment and started to change the way I talked about it.

It occurred to me that I wasn't a good fit at that other position. Maybe I was a better fit when I was there 15 years ago, but I'm too strong-willed, too independent for that job. My spiritual life had finally started to catch up. So, I was free to look and find something better suited, where I would be able to both explore my love of choral music, my spirituality, and my handyman skills at the same time. My ability to sit at a desk and prepare both good classroom activities and positively motivate faculty to prepare assessment plans no longer mattered. I didn't have to wear a badge. In fact, other than the computer systems I set up, I no longer log on to a corporate protected portal or use an employee ID number.

The internet is full of long, articulately written blog posts of people who quit academia. They were incensed by the tumultuousness of the job search, crushed by the abject loneliness and constant threat of job loss, tired of the discrimination because they didn't look, act, speak, or write the way they were supposed to. They fell in love with subject matter that inspired them to pursue advanced degrees, only to find the reality of a dream job

103

– with tenure – meant shopping at cheaper big box stores, going hungry to pay student loans, and working late into nights and weekends only to be judged by a nebulous set of criteria that seemed disingenuous.

What did that screaming boss do? He caused me to look at my life. It seemed that the universe had been saying that I need to do something that better matched my abilities. I was freed from a career which, though I loved, stopped me from growing or having a family. It shackled me with constant fear of failure.

I had been committed to a life of small towns, single, alone, living from paycheck to paycheck as I watched other professors drive their "vintage" 20-year-old cars, live in tiny apartments and struggle to pay their bills, while we argued about learning outcomes. Teaching was intensely fun, but it wasn't the only part of being a professor.

One day, a man came along and freed me from my old ideas. I didn't have to follow that path anymore. When I knew I would be fired, I sought out the advice of a friend. I told him I wanted to become a music minister, full time. My friend looked at me and said with his resonant voice, "I think you would make a hell of a music minster."

I jumped off. I never looked back. Here's my keys – it's been real. Thank God for the people in my life those days that led me into a better way.

NOTE #23

STAY IN TODAY

C an we plan something together? I love to stop and think about the future. What am I going to be doing on September 24th? What is going to happen next week? When am I going to get to take my next trip, and where?

All this future-projecting must be fun because I do it all the time. On New Year's Eve, as people exploded fireworks outside my house and I sat in bed with two panting dogs, I looked up places to go next July Fourth where fireworks are illegal, and dogs are allowed.

Unfortunately, when I exist in the future I no longer am in the moment. I get overwhelmed, because I think of what I need to do now to get me ready for later. I get confused because I may not be fully prepared.

Sometimes, when I'm working on something that requires tools (like a house project) I *really* project into the future, thinking of what the next steps need to be (why look at the directions?) and how I can plan to get there. This seems so innocent! It's just "planning for advanced outcomes." Do I have enough screws? Do I have enough bolts? Is the wood the right kind? Are my measurements correct? These are all great questions for planning, but it means that I am awful to deal with when in the middle of a physical project.

What if, instead of planning ahead, I just did the next thing? Got screws? Check. Got wood for shelves? Check. Got a tape measure? Check. Saw? Check. Have I got a plan already put together before I got the tools out?

Maybe this time I won't throw a tantrum like a seven-year-old because I've misplaced the tape measure – again.

How can we stay in the moment? Here are some things I try to do:

1. I try to look at my feet and take in exactly where I am. Is it hot or cold? Are there a lot of people? Are there more items that I need right now? Did I get them?
2. Am I aware of my body: my breath, shoulders, hands, feet, neck and back? Am I hunched over while I'm walking?
3. Have I slipped into thinking about the future?
4. Am I enjoying being in this moment?

One day I was waiting to get my hair cut and I did what I always automatically do: I pulled my phone out to read articles or play solitaire. This time, I stopped. I put the phone away, allowing my mind to wander as I looked out over the street. I marveled at the clouds forming as the rain was closing in. I thought of my day and focused on trying to relax my shoulders. I practiced my breathing and tried to calm my mind. By the time I walked into the hair salon, I was focused.

How can we best stay in the moment? After all, now is the only time we really have. When we start looking forward into the future, we're ignoring the great gift that is the present.

NOTE #24

DRIVE THE BUS

J ust drive the bus," he says. Except no one reminded him that I'm a choir director, not a bus driver.

A former pastor used to say this phrase, especially when it came to getting upset about someone in the church. Since I was the church choir director, I remained keenly aware of members joining and leaving.

I run a church music program. People come and go from the church; people come and go from the chorus, but the general trend always seems to point upward.

I'm a trained classical musician with a background in conducting and choral music literature who went to school many years. I used to teach courses about classical music, give stern warnings to budding composers about not using second inversion chords, and assured many people that moveable do solfege and the rhythm syllables of Edwin Gordon were the best way to teach music reading.

Today my position occasionally involves conducting and working with choirs, and more often it consists of working with personalities and shepherding volunteers. Some tell me that volunteers are easier; they *want* to be here. Some tell me that students are easier; they *must* be here. Neither are wrong.

When I taught school I had a captive audience – sort of. They got to choose whether they came to rehearsal. Most of the time, they did, but sometimes they would miss, and I would see them in the hallways or in other buildings a few hours later. I might have felt a little bit smug that I caught them! Volunteers, though, if they don't come, they don't necessarily give reasons. Sometimes their reasons are frivolous or silly. Other times, they are serious.

"Just drive the bus," Jon kept saying.

Teaching school choirs and leading volunteer choirs have a lot in common. In both cases, their time is important. They both want to do a good job, or they wouldn't have joined. Both attract people who like making a difference. Both consist of people with a love of music and of being together. In fact, sometimes people love being in the choir because they don't have to reveal too much of themselves to belong to a group.

Then, one day, someone leaves. "It's not you; it's me," they proclaim. Maybe they have a new conflict. Maybe a parent is ill, or a child needs additional help.

Maybe they just don't like rehearsals.

There are multiple reasons why people volunteer, and why they stay.

1. A volunteer feels needed.

People love to feel like they make a difference. I tell my choir, "Thank you for a great rehearsal." Of course, in a musical organization, if they feel like they are positively contributing, they keep coming back. Often, I pair newbies with someone experienced, asking them to sit together to establish a bond and indoctrinate them into the routine.

2. Their job is clear.

Volunteers stay because they have a clearly defined "job." Their job may be to come to rehearsals, sharpen pencils, make coffee, or buy supplies. People tend to stay if they have a job to do and don't feel overwhelmed. Also, they know when that job ends.

3. They may have other priorities, but that's okay.

Everyone needs a vacation, has a relative who needs them, an anniversary, birthday, or other significant event that causes them to miss. No problem! Tell them how much you'll miss them! Everyone is entitled to a life of their own.

4.   *They don't have to run the entire show.*

One of my flaws is to try and run everything. For most volunteers, this isn't the case.   Giving a lot of people smaller jobs engages more people. That being said, a few people like to have larger jobs, so that they feel like they can leave their mark on the volunteer program.

5.   *Their motivation may not be the same as yours.*

Recently, I volunteered at the church food drive and discovered that some of the hardest workers are the school kids. Their main motivation is to accrue hours for honor society. Which is better? Who cares! If people are there, their motivation doesn't matter.

As COVID-19 struck the world, my choir went from faithful and dependable to online-only in the blink of an eye.   Recently, we reminded each other how things changed so quickly. Remember when they quit letting people in the grocery store? Remember when the malls and schools closed? Remember when we were all stuck at home for months, where our lives had been somewhat normal just one day earlier?

As someone who works with volunteers, I'm faced with the constant pull of people's responsibilities versus their attraction to my musical programs. I also had to learn that ultimately, we are all just temporary.

I learned to quit taking it personally when someone couldn't volunteer because of some important occasion in their life. They wanted to be there, and if they had to miss, they respected me enough to let me know. I kept my door open to listen. In short, I started saying yes. It's not because they don't like me or want nothing to do with the choir. They are just leading lives too, and I've learned to be more understanding.

When we are in charge, especially of volunteers, we are like bus drivers. Sometimes, people like riding the bus. They like the people who go with them on the journey. Some people ride the bus regularly for whatever reason. Ultimately, it's a bus; people get on the bus, and they get off the bus.

"Just drive the bus," says Pastor Jon.

Simple and elegant, it takes away my need to explain everyone else's actions.

We don't have to be in charge today. Just drive the bus.

NOTE #25

ALLOW EXTRA TIME

Just this morning, I read an article about a woman who, decided that because of the Coronavirus, she would take the train from Boston to San Francisco. I took the train once: from Walnut Ridge, Arkansas to Chicago's Union Station. It was a long, 11-hour trip in coach. The train picked us up in the middle of the night after waiting in a small, pink room with bright fluorescent lighting. People stood around with backpacks and suitcases, looking anxiously up and down the tracks for the train headlight that would soon cut into the dark night. Thanks to delays, the northbound and southbound trains crossed at that small station, doubling the number of passengers and onlookers waiting to be whisked away.

Though I kept to myself as I waited to board the coming train, I was amazed at the number of people. I had never been on a long-distance train in the US before, and just assumed most people flew. Here, in the middle of the night, at a tiny station, were dozens of people heading toward Chicago.

The train came up, and, just like that, we stepped aboard. Cozy and warm, the train was wider than a bus and more comfortable than a plane. With blue accents and dimmed overhead lights, it was a challenge to find my place. I found my seat next to a hair stylist and off we went. Our long journey through the night started with a quick nap in a rather large chair – more akin to first class than coach.

Though an airplane would have gotten us there much faster, this was much more relaxed – no TSA checks, no separation of liquids, gels and aerosols, no shoes off, no luggage check-ins or long lines; just stand up, get on, and go.

During that cold day in November, I rode through corn fields, past rivers, hills, and valleys. I got up out of my chair, walked what seemed like miles from one train car to the next, and read. The train rocked back and forth, slowly churning its way up to Chicago. I didn't have to keep my eyes on the road, speed down freeways, or read signs. In fact, I didn't have to do much. I arrived in Chicago right in the center of town and never needed to park my car. The trip was slower, but I got to experience the forests of southern Illinois as they meld into the cornfields.

I have encountered others who share the wonder of long-distance train travel, of how much calmer and easier it is, and of how this overlooked method of travel is returning to fashion. The spaciousness of the train, the different landscapes, and relaxing all have great appeal, especially during social distancing.

In some ways, we yearn for slowdowns. RV sales and rentals recently skyrocketed. People are exploring national parks and camping out in the wilderness. Partially, they do this to avoid catching the coronavirus, but also because we long for respite.

When the world shut down in March 2020, I watched some struggle with aloneness, lose their identity without the daily grind of work, and struggle with the absence of friends or relatives. Some adjusted quickly and worked from home. Others found hobbies and interests to pass the time. My email inbox came alive with messages from former students and old friends from the past. I got a bike. I read and wrote more, and I took more time to think.

A few months ago, I came across a news story about "forest bathing," or what the Japanese call *shinrin-yoku.* What could the possible effectiveness be of walking around in a forest? I thought.

I asked my husband to go along, and he reluctantly agreed, if it wasn't too far away. I had already googled it: the nearby state forest (that I'd never heard of before) was only about 10 miles up the freeway from our house.

My husband's reluctancy mirrored my own reticence. What a waste of time! Where was the parking lot? Would other people there have masks on?

Despite all of this, off we went in my little car, headed to the state forest. The crowded parking lot didn't seem to bode well for our forest bathing adventure. How can one feel connected to nature when there are people all around?

Half-heartedly we went down a trail and into the tall pine trees. As the parking lot disappeared, the sounds of the highway grew dimmer and the gentle crunch of pine needles, dirt and rocks carried us deeper into the forest. We walked to a small ravine, water trickling through it. It was clear water, not the usual brown gunk that's more common in Southeast Texas bayous. In fact, this ravine was hidden by a canopy of trees. There were palm trees along the floor, deciduous trees, birds, and, since it was winter, few insects.

My attention was focused on the overwhelming amount of life around me. Instantly, the problems and concerns of tomorrow or yesterday seemed far away. There was only right here, in the forest, with the trees.

Surprisingly, the ride home seemed calmer. No longer worried about which lane to use to drive fastest on this busy Houston freeway, I let the car drive and I rode along, gently nudging it here and there, just being part of the freeway flow. The forest had worked, bringing me into a focused state where I stayed, for a short time, in the moment.

When we remain in the present, all sorts of amazing things happen, including surprise at just what is already around us. Was it really that important to get home quickly? Is it that important to fly to Chicago or rush around in my daily grind to get things done? How often do we overlook opportunities because we're too focused on getting through the day?

If there's one lesson to all of this, it's that extra time can bring extraordinary results.

NOTE #26

BE STILL AND KNOW

Tomi was one of my best friends. In fact, one of the reasons I bought my first house was because it was located just five doors away from hers. We were a community of two – visiting one another often, spending time together before or after work, laughing and joking, and telling stories. Tomi was family.

Tomi worked in a snack bar in the evenings. She earned a minimum wage and struggled to pay her rent and utility bills every month, but somehow had enough money to enjoy cable TV. She drove an old Ford Taurus, smoked like there was no tomorrow, and was a good Catholic who went to church.

Often, when I would visit her, she'd be in front of the TV, book in hand. Though she had no formal training, Tomi wanted to be a detective, often reading true crime mysteries while in the background Judge Judy, Judge Joe Brown, or Criminal Minds played day and night. Though she was always ready to go "junking" (antique shopping) or visiting "the bobble head store" (used clothing store), she never went anywhere without a wig and would often tell others how almost everything about her was fake: fake hair, fake nails.

One thing that was not fake was her personality.

Tomi believed that most people were redeemable. She would spend hours talking on the phone to women who needed help, calmly urging them to do the right thing. She spent even more time supporting her granddaughters, of whom she was extremely proud.

Most of all, Tomi, who had gone from having nice clothes and a nice house to living in a shack and working minimum wage jobs, had learned the importance of humility. She didn't act as though the world owed her something. Instead, she spoke honestly and quietly. If something weren't right, she would say it; and then she'd do something about it, including walking away from it.

She loved working with others from the comfort of her living room and often spent hours counseling either our students, her granddaughters, or some of the many women who looked up to her. She spoke elegantly and earnestly, and people respected her because she told the truth.

In short, Tomi stayed in the moment.

Even after she was diagnosed with cancer, she didn't discuss what would happen in the future, or who would watch her house, or what others should do when she was gone. Instead, she focused on the moment. Tomi made choices: radiation only, shrink the tumor, then surgery. She never worried about getting rides to the local cancer center.

Remaining in the present poses all sorts of challenges. How will we be ready for the future? How can we accept the things that are happening now? How do we face uncertainty and maybe even our own demise?

My friend showed us how.

With dignity, grace and faith, Tomi demonstrated what she talked about for years working with others showed: that God takes care of us, especially in our final hours. Being Catholic, Tomi brought out her rosary, prayed fervently, and accepted that this life would likely end soon.

Faith was never an abstract notion for Tomi. It was a practical necessity that informed her decision process. Though she lived in a secular world surrounded by students and faculty, occasionally she would make comments about scripture that spoke volumes to her knowledge of the Bible. "Read a portion of the Psalms and Proverbs daily," she'd say. "If you want to know more about the church, read Acts." "If a man sues you for your shirt, give him your coat as well," she'd quote.

In fact, she quoted scripture so regularly that it inspired many of us that knew her to get Bibles.

One of the phrases she quoted most often was "God is not the author of chaos and confusion. He's the source of peace," which is a paraphrase from 1 Corinthians. She would then correlate that phrase: so that means if I feel confused, I'm not with God.

Those of us who would go to her for advice often heard this phrase, rather than get specific advice. It allowed us to make our own choices, informed by what we thought were the profound words of Tomi, rather than the writings of Paul. If we didn't know what to do, still, she offered this from scripture:

"Be still and know."

God comes in small moments, surprises, and insights. In fact, only when our voices are silent – when we remain still – do we get to hear that small voice, leading us out of fear.

Teaching us to walk by faith.

NOTE #27

MAKE A CHANGE BY BEING A CHANGE

In my first evaluation at Cypress Creek Christian Church, my senior pastor wrote "as you grow into your new position, always keep in mind that your presence reminds people of the change."

I marveled at the profoundness of this concept. Just walking in the room was a change. When I started rehearsal, before I moved one chair or picked one new anthem, I made a change by *showing up*. Even if I mimicked everything that the previous director does, I created a change. I didn't like to have casual conversations during business meetings. I printed rehearsal orders with times. I told jokes. I let anyone in my choir – anyone. In this and so many more ways, I was different.

I created change in other ways too. I knew a little about technology and handy work. I spoke well and listened terribly. I worked hard at other, non-musical tasks around the church.

Then something else happened: new people started coming. Some came back. Some talked about how they like rehearsals. They're fun, they say, and yet hard work.

Some told me how they didn't know if the church would go on when the former director left. They told me they didn't think I would be able to fill the role.

Then the flood came.

In 2017, our church took on so much water that only one room in the entire campus was spared. Floors were gutted; toys, chairs, Bibles, hymnals, walls, electrical, and everything was mucked out and removed. Over the course of three years, our choir continued – first in another church, then in a restored chapel, and then in a new choir room in another building. We endured changes and weathered each crisis.

Now, with our last building finished, we have all changed. We got used to the smaller worship space. We changed offices. We restarted our craft show. We moved bells and rehearsed in another room. We adapted.

These past years caused the church to grow, and me as well. Everything that was handed to me – the rehearsal rooms, the worship space, even the carpet, are gone, and we had to reinvent ourselves. Two of us emptied closets full of forty years of junk. We set aside workdays where everything was moved to other buildings. Movers took our entire choir library – hundreds of boxes – down flights of stairs and into a new space that had been carefully measured to fit. Instead of restoring things the way they were, we asked, "how can we make this better?" We added new technologies. We repurposed old closet space, paid off debts, strengthened our financial standing, and worshipped closer together.

How can we act as the change?

1. *We acknowledge that change has occurred.*

What kind of changes are happening? It could be age-related, getting a new pet, moving, or a change in relationships. What kind of stress has occurred because of this?

2. *We react kindly and gently to the change.*

Can we still find time to exercise, eat right, and talk with others about our worries and anticipations of the future? Do we remain kind to ourselves?

3. *We don't play "the victim."*

Each of us has friends who support us by standing in our corner. Though empathy is important, we must acknowledge our own path. What part did we play in this change? Though our commiserating friends are more fun to talk to, our rational-thinking friends can provide perspective and solutions that we need.

4.   *We aim for a new perspective.*

Review the change as it happens. How have things improved? Is there something good that came out of this change? Though it may be difficult to go through, is life better? If not, what set this into motion?

When I first moved to Spring, the change was instant. I sold my home and the house I was trying to buy fell through. I worked, prayed, and went to the gym. I spoke with friends and spiritual advisers who helped me see things clearly, gave good advice, and reminded me that I would love this new way of life. Finally, I looked at the bigger picture – a nicer job, less time alone, and better musical opportunities were within reach.

Everything changed; as a result, my perspective changed, too.

NOTE #28

D.I.Y. JUST FOR F.U.N.

The car repair cost me about $500.

In January 2014, I found myself underneath a car, changing out an alternator. I had only changed an alternator once, and never on a foreign car. With space heaters on in a well-lit garage, I laid first underneath, then above the engine. By now I had already begun looking over the tops of my glasses because I can't see anything close-up anymore.

"Hold the light over here," I heard myself say; sounding more and more like my dad each time.

How difficult can this be? Undo a few bolts, exchange the alternator, close the bolts, finish!

Well, I found out.

I had to take out the battery, take out the air filter, then take out the wheel (because the alternator is on the side of the engine and to get to that last bolt, one must remove the drivers' side front wheel.)

I cursed at this thing – why did I agree to do this again? It's a mitzvah, I told myself, a good deed.

Finally, all buttoned up, the car ran again perfectly. We charged the battery one more time, and vroom! Off the car went! It was a success, and I was proud at the work I had done.

Two weeks later the battery died.

Disgusted, my regular mechanic told me it was the alternator. Apparently, I had not installed the alternator correctly, so, two weeks later, I bought a new alternator.

Sometimes it's best to let an expert handle a job, but sometimes it's fun to DIY it too. Experts do it right the first time, but DIY gives us a chance to grow. After all, don't we best learn by failing?

Once, when out of work, I was hired by a friend to help fix houses to rent. I had no idea what I was doing and had a great time the entire way. None of us was in construction as a first job, so a lot of my newbie errors were overlooked or tolerated. Doing these repairs on houses gave me the confidence to do my own home projects – running new pipe, adding electrical work, painting, adding sinks and tiles, installing bathtubs, and covering walls in sheet rock. I learned a lot, enjoyed it, and it kept me from sitting in the house.

I can change car air filters, add low voltage lighting inside and out, and even build a fence or two. I love working with my hands because there is a tangible change in the state of things. More than that, it reminds me of "holding the light" for my father as a child, and it makes me feel connected to his memory.

But some things are best left to the professionals. When a tree in the backyard fell during a spring storm, I called a professional. When my car started to overheat, I didn't try to replace the heater hoses myself, because they required special tools and special parts. Instead, I paid for the professional.

Though often I will try to do the work myself if I can, some things I still need a professional to do. Sometimes being of service to others doesn't mean fixing it. It means giving someone else a chance to earn money.

Today, there are businesses that will literally help with anything. Need to run to the store? There's a business for that. Need a ride? There's an app. Need a new car? There's a business that will negotiate one for you online.

But when I go outside in the mornings with the dogs and I look at my air-conditioning compressor, still humming away after I fixed the old fan motor, I feel a sense of accomplishment and pride. The guy at the HVAC repair place could have done it much faster, but I smile because I did it myself.

The number of benefits of DIY projects are amazing, but here are some:

1. It saves money.

I can't even begin to fathom the amount of money I've saved from doing some of my own repair. The air conditioner repairs alone probably cost about $1500. Replacing a car cabin air filter would have been about $80. New built-in shelving in the front room could have easily run me $1000.

2. It boosts confidence.

When I installed outdoor party lights across my backyard, little did I know that I would reuse those same skills over and over in installing lights in my attic, plugs on the outside of the house, ballasts at the church, and lighting in my shelves. Though I still feel I am terrible at "fishing" wires, my accuracy and comfortability with this has improved dramatically.

3. It reduces stress.

The first moments of a new DIY project were so agonizing. As I brought the tools out of the garage, I thought to myself "I'll never get this done."

I think that until starting the very first mound of dirt.

Once I start, I relish in the work, joyful at the opportunity to be outside for a long period of time. At the end of the day, I have something to show for my trouble. I don't think about work or worship, just digging, or cementing, or leveling posts.

4. It's great exercise.

Though some projects are tougher than others, most require some strength and endurance. If I don't have it, I take a few more breaks, but by then my mind focuses completely on the work at hand, just like it does in a strenuous workout.

5. It gives a sense of pride.

When people come to my house, the first thing they notice are all the antiques on the walls and the lovely built-in bookcase. "We made that," I get to say. I get to tell them how we cut the wood, screwed it into the frame of the house, and fitted the bookcase exactly into the wall. I show off the fountains I built, and I explain how I used a diamond-head hole saw, where I bought the pump, and how I looked for weeks for just the right container to go with the ceramic bowl.

If it seems too dangerous, I hire the professionals. I don't climb up into the rafters to change out stage lights, cut limbs off trees with chainsaws, or rewire my home's circuit panel, but for home projects, I'm all in.

…except for changing alternators. I'm never doing that again.

NOTE #29

PITCH IN. IT'S ALWAYS WORTH IT

Watching one of those home-rehab shows, I saw something that absolutely frustrates me. Sod was placed in front of the wrong house and as the protagonist team of house-flippers came onto the scene, they questioned the foreman about it. The foreman, not one of the main characters, folded his hands, proclaimed, "They sent it to the wrong house. They'll have it next week," and declared he was leaving the site.

How much of this is scripted? I thought.

It can be frustrating when people say, "I can't!" and give up.

How often do our attitudes like this impact our actions?

1. Is it I can't, or I won't?

Sometimes, we get trapped into believing our own ability is less than it is. Marianne Williamson says:

> *Our deepest fear is not that we are*
> *inadequate. Our deepest fear is that we are*
> *powerful beyond measure.*

Sometimes we say, "I can't" instead of "I don't want to."

2. Is it someone else's responsibility?

Sometimes we're faced with the possibility that a job is not in our purview. We always must be careful not to take from someone else their job, whether we could do it better or not. We must allow others to do their part, while also being helpful, if needed.

3. Do I need more confidence?

"Can't" comes from a lack of confidence sometimes. Is there a similar task that we have done that could prepare us for this one? Are there some tasks that we can accomplish? What ramifications will happen if we fail?

4. Sometimes it just can't be done.

In the above reality-tv show, the sod was delivered and installed at another house. It can't be un-installed. In that case, it required starting over.

My choir hosts a contest for non-varsity (non-competitive) choirs every spring. I've gotten to know some of the directors since they come to our contest year after year. This particular year, one of the usual schools had a new director. He was kind and soft-spoken, and his students seemed to genuinely like him.

At 7AM the day before the contest, I received a phone call from the new director, telling me that he was running a little late but would be there, ready to perform with his choir soon. As I listened to the voicemail, a horrible realization came to me that this man was bringing his students now – *today* – a day early. He had already procured a bus, collected permission slips, corralled his students onto that bus, and was driving to my church to do this contest in front of judges.

Except that this was Thursday. The contest was on Friday.

I had that sick feeling of knowing that this man's day was about to become a disaster when I called him back to tell him.

Then the thought crossed my mind – *why not make it today too?* I raced home, grabbed a suit and tie and some nice shoes, and drove quickly to the church, calling him back along the way. "No problem! Take your time," I said.

As I reached the church, I quickly brought my suit in to the office and began arranging the chairs, moving the piano, bringing out the recording equipment, and turning on the lights.

I quickly changed out of my casual morning clothes into my suit and tie and began calling people close by who could judge the contest.

I found the church secretary and, since she had a degree in vocal music, deputized her as a judge. The students came in, I handled the recording equipment, judged, and sent them home with comments and a good recording of their performance. Though his choir wasn't eligible for the "Best in Class" competition, we made it work for him as best we could with a couple of hours' notice.

Why did I go through so much trouble to accommodate his error? I could have explained to the director that he had the wrong date; to come back tomorrow, but I had walked in shoes like his. I knew how exhausting it is to get students out of class, get a bus and driver, make a two-hour trek across the city, arrange chaperones, hire an accompanist, teach the music, and finally direct the choir without any of them misbehaving. When I told him that he had gotten the date wrong, I could hear the beginnings of despair as a weak "Ok...." sounded in my phone headset.

I said, "Don't worry about it; we'll fix it." I couldn't imagine telling this man after all of that he had to turn around.

There are times when it's important to say no, but sometimes it's equally important to say yes. It wasn't that difficult to move a bunch of chairs, and with a little help, I had judges' tables and a recording space ready in no time. So why not? If it's in my power, why not allow this choir to receive comments and ratings? There was no reason to deny his students the experience of the competition.

It could be argued that it wasn't right; that he needed to come on the correct day. This person's choir competed in a special session, with different judges, on an alternate day, with no possibility of receiving "Best in Class." When weighing the "next right thing," it meant adding a bit of work to accommodate someone else's mistake. Maybe because I had spent time teaching school and bringing kids to contests that I knew the herculean effort he had taken and wasn't about to let him go home empty-handed. I pitched in and helped.

NOTE #30

UNDERSTAND YOUR INNER SABOTEUR

The first two figures of Richard Strauss's *Don Juan* are hauntingly difficult. They are also the beginning of a roller coaster for conductors. It begins off-beat, seems to destabilize any rhythm, and to make it worse, it starts on a rest!

It really is a nightmare.

For the conductor, the real challenge still lies ahead.

In Romania, I was in front of the orchestra. I hit the first downbeat, moved through the opening tumult, approached the sudden change of tempo, and failed to keep the orchestra together.

Less is more, I've always been taught. As I approached the slow measures, I didn't subdivide the beat, and BAM! The orchestra wasn't together.

Fortunately, this was a closed rehearsal. Maestro Balan, the orchestra director, walked up to me. I knew what was coming.

"Why didn't you subdivide??? Why???" It was a friendly inquiry with a smile, and yet it included a twinge of rebuke – just enough to make me want to crawl under the podium.

The rebuke was well deserved. After all, I was responsible for the poor performance in my attempt to conduct the piece.

I had been terrified. I seized up, knowing I could fail at this. Eventually I went out and did so.

After talking with Balan about the issue, he released me to try again. This time I sailed through it. In fact, the next week, when I conducted Shostakovich and Brahms, I knew if it didn't work, I could do it again. I was still learning, and I wasn't perfect. Maestro Balan or Maestro Gutter would stop me, pull me aside, suggest a solution, and I would continue.

As rehearsals moved ahead, I became more comfortable about trusting my own instincts – learning to stop when the tempo changed, staying out of my score, and watching the players instead of remaining in my head.

In fact, the day I crashed the orchestra, other than my own recollection, it was a non-incident. To everyone else, it was just part of the rehearsal process. No one suffered, no one died, and now, years later, probably no one else remembers. The failure came down to one issue – fear.

Fear sometimes keeps us from doing what we want or need to do.

I get nervous before every concert, every speaking event, every rehearsal, every workshop that I lead. It is a normal part of my existence. Knowing that most of the time, I get to redo a mistake brings me great comfort. All I need to do is make it to the stage, classroom, sanctuary, rehearsal, or whatever, and start with note number one. From there, it's no longer about me. It's not my problem to deal with anymore. Instead, it is the music that's at the forefront, and I am the servant. I have a job to do. I am here to create music.

My internal issues are not just related to music and performance. They reveal themselves anytime I'm experiencing something new.

A few weeks ago, the associate minister asked me if I would put some plugs above her desk like we had in our office. So, I set out, multitool in hand, to buzz through the drywall and start the installation of her new plugs. After I cut out the hole, I noticed she had insulation between the walls, and I needed to fish through that insulation to get to the new hole that I had just cut out. It took me forever. I sweated profusely. I worried and thought about how this wasn't going to work; how she'd have to put a picture over it, and how I cut holes in her pretty office wall.

Looking around the church, I found a wire hanger by the choir robes, fished the wire, and went back to the store only once to get a set of fancy steel boxes that, with a little clip, connected to the drywall, creating a new electrical haven for plugs, chargers, and anything else.

Fear kept stopping me until I realized I had a job to do. Fear overwhelmed me, stopping my work on the plugs. Fear prevented me from using a divided beat to bring the orchestra successfully through the slow measures of *Don Juan.* Fear kept me from a whole host of other things, until I learned to respect it, accept it, and ignore it.

Ultimately, when we give in to fear, we grant power to the inner saboteur. The saboteur wrecks us. It convinces us that since we weren't "born" with that innate talent that we can never possess the skill. It turns us away from adventures and ideas. It causes us to listen to the judgmental voice designed to keep us "safe."

The saboteur does this in the name of "protection." It wants us safe at all times. It doesn't want us to fail or get booed or ridiculed. But the saboteur also bars us from growth. It makes us quit trying to achieve better things for ourselves. It tells us that we're never going to be as good, as talented, as strong, as athletic, as musical, as artistic, or as articulate as "them." It protects us from failure by not allowing us to try.

The inner saboteur is deadly in its own way. It shields us from life's adventures. It mars us from taking risks. It convinces us to not travel those untrodden paths. It shows us that others' opinions are more important. All of this is done for self-protection.

Don't let the saboteur keep you "protected." It's just harming you in the end.

NOTE #31

RESIST THE STORM

Ever get mad?

At one school, my co-worker would come into my office with a forced smile, sit down, and tell me what new, silly thing our boss had done. Usually, this meant a conversation like:

"Your budget has been cut off."

"Your music scholarships are gone."

"You have to tour for a week around the USA with 50 kids and have two thousand dollars. How does Spring Break sound?"

"Finish your doctorate or find another job."

It was constant. I would come to school, mad about something that had been changed, or something out of my control. I'd scowl as I walked to my office, isolated.

My friends had families to go home to – spouses and children who walked with them through their life journey. I ate most of my meals alone, comforted in the fact that I had a job.

The thing I enjoyed in my life – my career – seemed in constant chaos. The number of students across the campus dwindled. Our retirement was cut, our health insurance became more and more expensive, and I started questioning. As I walked to school in the mornings, I felt angry – always angry.

Fortunately, my best friend's house was between mine and the office. I would stop in, tell her what new ridiculous thing had happened, and we'd shake our heads. Then she would tell me the latest story about one or both of her granddaughters. Eventually I forgot why I was mad.

Sometimes, though, the ideas would still fester and grow. Then, something happened, usually from a boss's new edict. Wanting to yell and scream, I pretended that I had a button, the "nuclear button."

Then I would brush that button off and put it away.

It wasn't easy. I didn't always do it, but the number of times I would get frustrated grew less and less the more I stayed away from the "nuclear button." Most people had no idea how often I endured yelling from administrators, or how difficult it was to maintain composure when faced with regular job threats.

One friend told me years later that "people aren't usually doing things *to* you, they're just doing things, and you're getting hurt in the process." I asked God to help me not be so angry all the time. As a result, I learned to start keeping my mouth shut.

The storms don't occur often anymore. Here's how I dealt with them.

1. Ask yourself, "Is this so important to disrupt my serenity?"

If the answer is no, quit worrying about it. After all, the universe will still unfold exactly the way it should.

2. Stay away from negative ideas.

For me, this means staying away from the news or Facebook and paying more attention to music. It means not interacting with people who bring me down and spending more time with those that I enjoy.

3. Take moments for yourself.

Talking to a friend on the phone, going for a walk, visiting a colleague in their office, or even spending a moment outside can help.

4. Vent with trusted friends or colleagues.

Sometimes it just feels better to express frustration and, in the process, make the other person laugh.

5. Keep perspective.

Most of us take a job for a goal, a career, or for doing something we love to do. Our jobs are a tool; they do not define us as human beings.

6. *Enjoy a life outside work.*

The work/life balance takes time to find, but without it, we're doomed.

7. *Find the true source of the anger.*

Often, I have found that my own anger has little to do with the reason in front of me and more to do with a past reminder, drama, or fear that the current situation barely touches.

There's a saying "if you spot it, you got it," meaning the things that really bother us touch a nerve about some insecurity or issue that is internal.

It seems like I get most enraged when I feel like my "rights" have been trampled. In my mind, getting what I want and being heard are my "rights."

Even in the worst possible disparagement and the worst situation we get to make the choice to react or ignore it. Sometimes, we can think about something else or do something that makes us happy.

I have a choice to say something or not. Inside I may be furious. I may look up to God in my head and scream, "FIX THIS!! ARE YOU THERE???" And in that, I found my new, hidden superpower.

Saying nothing.

Turning away is so profound, so charged, so amazing, that if we yield to it, even clumsily, it has more of an effect than yelling ever did. If we react, the other person knows exactly my feeling and intent, but when we say nothing, the interpretation falls back on the other person.

People judge us by our actions, not our feelings. When something is bothering me, and it doesn't have to do with the person in front of me, I try to keep my mouth shut now. It's not their fault. When I don't give in to the temptation to go off on someone, I don't have to apologize later. When I'm hurt by someone, I'm equipped with the even more profound gift; the gift of saying nothing.

NOTE #32

DON'T JUST GO. BOLDLY GO

My favorite type of travel involves driving. Getting behind the wheel, anticipating each mile, and listening to music all evoke a fantasy of freedom for me. Years ago, I discovered if I wanted to visit places, I needed to quit waiting for others to make plans with me. I was used to flying back and forth when I was in school, so I was accustomed to flying by myself.

In the early 2000's I started taking solo trips. At first, it was a novelty. I started exploring cities – Chicago, Denver, Dallas, Seattle, Portland, San Francisco, LA or wherever I could get a reasonable fare. Usually, I went to watch the symphony as the main attraction, but also just to get out of town. On those trips, I read, I kept to myself, and I saw museums, the opera, concerts, parks, and nature.

What's the greatest thing I learned? Traveling alone almost never meant being alone. At most places, my phone seemed to jingle more than at home. Sometimes I had great conversations with total strangers.

If you haven't traveled solo before, here are some tips to prepare:

1. Start by evaluating where you wish to go and why.

Is it curiosity? Is there a desire to visit something spectacular? Is it a writing, spiritual or work retreat? Is there a workshop at the destination? Find a reason – however minimal – to go.

2. Start simple.

Practice taking yourself out to dinner. Take a shopping trip alone. Go to the nearest bookstore to read something. Attend a concert or museum exhibit by yourself. Feel the awkwardness that eventually vanishes as the concert, exhibit, or meal happens. Bring a book to read or a notepad to write during those moments where the alone time is especially poignant. Read columns about other solo travelers and watch YouTube videos about traveling by yourself.

3. Try a "mini-trip."

Bring a camera, a phone, a list of places to visit, and travel to a nearby city for an overnight stay. Combine it, if you wish, with a visit to see relatives before or after.

Use that information to know what to pack and bring on a longer trip.

4. Stay in touch.

Let others know when you're going and check in regularly. Every time I have left town, I'm amazed at how much more time I spend talking to people from home when I'm not there.

5. Try overseas travel too.

Going overseas, while requiring a little more planning, can be just as fun. Get some guidebooks of the country you will visit. Rip pages out with maps and keep them in your pocket. Don't speak the language? No problem! Find a way to update your phone to use Google Translate, or carry a phrase book. Ask questions of others who've been there.

The bottom line is, don't let fear keep you from traveling alone just because you won't have anyone to talk to. Have an itinerary or an agenda (photography, concerts, natural or historical sites) and do it.

Never be afraid to go.

NOTE #33

WATCH HOW GOD WORKS

Working on a virtual fall event for the church with other staff, we experimented with "breakout rooms" in the virtual meeting space. As we started our conversation, we had all kinds of complicated ideas to define the upcoming online project. We were going to have classes and events and long discussions over the online platform.

Since we were new to the technology, we needed to practice how to use breakout rooms. As we practiced creating these "rooms," we found a discussion prompt waiting for us.

"What is the thing you appreciate most in your physical space?"

Though just a test prompt, one staff member and I, the test subjects in our technological maze, looked around our digital boxes on the screen like some sort of knock-off *Brady Bunch* group. We found items nearby and shared about them.

We were tired of social distancing, zoom and technology, and it seemed like another terrible exercise of fake human "contact." Nonetheless, we tried.

Now I had no intention of detailing my insecurities, my fears, or my passions. Truthfully, I don't necessarily like revealing too much of my personal life at work and I am drawn to others who feel this way. Yet here was an innocuous question – talk about an object. Not me, not my emotions, but an object.

So, we started. She showed me a painting that one of the youths had given to her. It was creative, thoughtful, and well-crafted by a child that I didn't know had an artistic eye.

I showed my lamp – built by a previous pastor. It uses a wooden base, light socket with a small tube bulb, and a Hemmingray glass insulator – the green globe used in old telephone and telegraph lines. For a while, the pastor had preached on images of light used in Jesus' story, and in the process of this, created several lamps as part of the sermon series. I was moved by this gift because the pastor had created it himself, and because it represented a set of sermons. It indicated a level of thought and preparation and is a touching memory of our short time together in ministry.

As I explained this, my co-worker and I shared events in our lives that had meaning for each of us. We found out more about each other because we'd revealed ourselves just a little bit.

This is the way God works: subtly, gently, creating events and experiences that we have with one another. These events are shared and never occur in a vacuum. We discovered one another's humanity accidentally, one moment at a time. A little innocuous question about the stuff in our current zoom location and, by accident, we found a common bond. Together, we returned outside the breakout room. We had our answer as to how to engage our congregation members. Gently and quietly, we provided experiences to reveal more about ourselves.

In 1996, I drove to New Jersey and found my way to the student center of my new graduate school. Together with one of my close friends, Mark, we had made the long trek from Houston. While looking at the bulletin board for odd jobs, I lamented to Mark that I would no longer be in his temple choir.

A woman with dark, curly hair heard me say this. Walking up to us, she asked if I had sung in a synagogue before.

"Yes," I responded. I introduced her to Mark, the organist and choir director of Temple Emanu-El of Fort Worth. Mark had introduced me to the wonders of synagogue choral music, along with Schenkerian Analysis and a love of music theory. Cantor Donna Faye, thrilled to meet us, asked me to sing for her, and immediately I was hired to sing at a synagogue in Livingston, about an hour's drive north of that school. I learned so much from regularly attending services there about my childhood religion and heritage. In short, through great singing, laughter, and a lot of great music I fell in love with reform Judaism. As graduation approached, I thought about changing course to go to cantorial school instead of a doctoral program in conducting.

Though I don't attend synagogues very often anymore, my love for Jewish music remains. Often, I use the improvisatory techniques in my singing in the church. I relate to my choir members' desire to bring more to the service, all because of a random incident so long ago.

In simple, subtle ways, God makes these wonderous connections that have profound impacts on our lives. This is how God works best: gently, quietly, showing us how our whole lives change with just one average moment.

NOTE #34

PRAY. IT'S GOOD FOR YOU

P eople say nice things about my prayers.

At a Thanksgiving potluck, all the usual food was ready: turkey, mashed potatoes, banana pudding, green beans, and whatever else there was from a group of about 40 and their families. Always a huge event, the annual Thanksgiving potluck drew people from all over.

As a music professor back in those days and no family nearby, I had no formal association with any church. Nonetheless, the organizer asked me to lead the prayer over the food.

As I started, a lady piped up, "EXCUSE ME," as she interrupted my prophetic waxing. Stomachs growled.

"I'D LIKE TO MAKE A SPECIAL REQUEST."

I don't know what I was thinking. It wasn't like we all had anywhere else to go; it was Thanksgiving, for goodness' sake. The local Wal-Mart wouldn't open for another four hours, the restaurants were closed, and the only thing there was to do was, well, eat.

Here was someone who had stopped the flow. Our host had already introduced us. Using the kindest voice, with plenty of sympathy, I blurted out.

"Sorry, this is just a general food blessing."

It became the joke of the potluck. Every year afterward, I was asked to give Joel's General Food Blessing. No specifics. No special requests tonight; just General Food Blessing.

Food blessings or not, prayer binds us to God. It's not our needs or wants. Nor is it a laundry list to God. It's an intentional moment we spend with the Almighty.

What kind of prayers support the spiritual flow? What interrupts it? What creates better connections to the divine? What do I want to hear, as a listener? Two types of prayers emerge: the *external* – prayer with others, and the *internal* – prayer with God alone.

Internal prayer is between God and I. I can say whatever I want. At the core, though, it's a "perpetual surrender to God," says Trappist monk Thomas Merton.

Prayer allows us *acceptance* of our current circumstances, recognizing that we don't get to decide fates or outcomes. Once we accept that our lives are not always in our control, we grow spiritually.

When I finally accepted that I could talk to God without muttering "thou arts" or "begats," my life began to change.

A few months ago, working with someone who has a lot of difficulty with prayer, I had a thought. Each day, we wrote to God something short. We each texted it to one another. I had a prayer journal that had been languishing in a drawer for years, untouched. Out came the journal and we agreed to write these daily prayers for one month.

What I discovered is that in those early hours of the morning, my mind seems to be most open. I write before checking email, before putting dishes away from the night before, and before taking the dogs out for the second time. We sit down together, me and God, at the kitchen table, and I write.

Sometimes, the writing rambles. Sometimes it works things out. Either way, for a few moments, I talk, I listen, and I write.

Sometimes I pray for others specifically, especially when I know they're going through hard times, or when they need some guidance. Sometimes it's thanks, and it helps me to stay centered and focused on the moment. Though I try to only pray for others, I'm amazed at how often my prayers still contain the word "I."

Shouldn't prayer be an act of thanksgiving? We acknowledge, through the act of prayer, that we are dependent upon God. By giving thanks, we are forced to state our own limitations, God's omnipotence, and see how God's Hand is present in all things in our lives.

There are five steps in my personal prayer life:

1. *Pray simply.*

Even the shortest request can be powerful. If I'm praying internally, it's not for others anyway.

2. *Pray regularly.*

I pray each morning when I first get up, and night, before I go to sleep. Despite being pawed at by dogs or distractions around me, I get on my knees. This started when I was at one of the low points in my life, and I tried it only when I had nothing else to lose. My life improved almost immediately.

3. *Pray expectantly.*

As I said before, God has three answers: "yes," "not right now," and "I have something better." It's "something better" that seems to keep happening. I never would have imagined my life would turn out the way it has, and it always seems to keep surprising me.

4. *Pray with the other senses.*

In the evenings I light candles. Sometimes I use ambient sounds – anything to get my mind off me for a minute.

5. *When all else fails, use a reading.*

There are so many books to use, that it's not necessary to reinvent the wheel. We all can't be spiritual giants every day. Sometimes that means let someone else do the heavy lifting and come up with the topic for prayer.

What about *external* prayer? When I pray for a group, this is when I feel closest to God. Here is what I do:

1. *Breathe.*
Allow the silence to inspire.

2. *Acknowledge.*
Make sure to note our dependence upon God.

3. *Offer thanks.*
This means give thanks for the day, for the meeting, for the choir, for the opportunity to see others, or any other thanks that is appropriate to the situation.

4. *Ask for God to intercede.*
One of the limits of intercession prayers is refraining from the word "I." I try to keep in mind that while I'm using my own words, the prayer is for everyone in the room.

5. *Ask God to show his will.*
Stay open to what that will is – whether I think it's good for me or not.

6. Last, ask God to send us out.

I make sure that end is positive, with hope, renewed spirit, or blessing.

7. End the prayer.

I use a little tag: "and all God's children said…" prompting the group to say "amen."

I don't know why this works, but I know that it does. In those moments of prayer, I feel as though we are collectively together.   More than choir directing, good music making, or a spectacular performance, I feel that praying with others is the most important thing I do.

NOTE #35

CHOOSE YOUR LEVEL OF
ALONENESS

After moving out of Texas, I found myself in a small town, burned up with resentment over a year I didn't ask for, and a future that I couldn't fathom.

My dad had died, a relationship ended, and my life changed. Speaking with my college choir director, I knew I needed a different position. The solution was clear: leave everyone behind. Move somewhere else. Start over.

So, I did.

In July, I moved – somewhat sure that this was where I was supposed to go. As a young professor, I knew to cast my net wide when looking for a job, and not be afraid to move places I normally wouldn't go. I moved from small town to smaller town, miles away from any major city. The landscape was beautiful – hills, four seasons, and plenty of stars at night. Yet my professional prospects seemed to vanish.

With no friends and few acquaintances, I settled into my solitary life. During the week I had classes to teach, papers to grade, and work to do. After dark, the town closed in. Though some friends came to visit from elsewhere, for the most part I was alone. I sometimes left my house in the evenings, wondering why I moved here, what good I was doing, and where I was going. A career and a life seemingly off the rails, I had no friends, no professional prospects, and no way to grow.

The building where I worked didn't bustle with anyone and by mid-afternoon filled with silence. I drove home to find a lonely house. On weekends, I would stay inside, certain that no one would ever miss me.

About seven months into self-imposed isolation the phone rang. No one ever called my phone. In those days I didn't own a cell phone. It was Roscoe, one of my new acquaintances. "Just calling to say hello," he said.

Roscoe was one of the happiest people I knew. He walked everywhere because he'd been blind since birth. He washed dishes at the local restaurant, perennially laughed about his experiences, and never seemed to let his alone time get to him.

More often, though, he reminded me that loneliness is a choice. I disagreed. I *deserved* to be apart from others; to be alone.

Paul says in Romans that "suffering leads to perseverance, perseverance to character, and character to hope." As time went on in my new surroundings, an odd thing happened: each Saturday around 2 or 3 in the afternoon Roscoe called. We met others in town, and soon the number of friends began to grow. For the first time, I felt like I belonged.

Roscoe showed how one doesn't have to be alone. As an introvert, I feel uncomfortable surrounded by others – even if it's others who share a lot of the same interests. With Roscoe, I learned more about the art of being a friend.

Judy Robinett, author of *How to Be a Power Connector*, says that most blockades for connecting with others comes down to fear. "I was never a connector or extrovert. I eventually found out many others are wonderful and if you focus on them, it numbs your fear."

Here are some ways I have found to connect with others.

1. *Watch the body language.*

Body language communicates a great deal. Am I on my phone? Am I looking at the ground or standing in a corner? Conductors monitor their body language during music making, and some of the same rules apply: shoulders back, head up, eyes forward and out of the music (or phone, or book.)

2. Shake hands and say hello.

This is deceiving, because saying, "How are you doing?" can be both inviting and stand-offish. It's inviting if I am looking in the eyes of the other person. It's a standoff if I'm walking by when I say it.

3. Ask the other person a question.

Take the focus off and put it on someone else by asking them a question. Don't ask "How's it going," or "How are you?" Both can be answered with one word, like "fine," and the conversation ends. If both you and the other person are from out of town, ask where they are from. If both of you are at an event, ask, "How do you know the host?"

4. Make a comment about the location or surroundings.

Awareness comes in handy. Does the person have a unique position or action? Are both of you waiting in line, or on a plane, or in the grocery store? Did your encounter happen at a conference or theater? Each of us can find things in common to help start a conversation.

5. Force yourself to listen.

My toughest challenge in any conversation is to not interrupt with a funny anecdote of my own. Once I do, I have moved the conversation to myself, and killed it.

Constantly consider questions about what the other person has said, to try and bring them out more.

6. Decide if you want to keep talking or move on.

Do you want to keep in touch with the other person after this conversation? Did you ask for their business card, email address, website, or phone number?

Maybe the person is not someone you need to engage with any further. In that case, say goodbye, knowing that you practiced the art of engaging.

The other day my husband and I visited the Gite Gallery, a trove of African art in a stylish, refurbished 1940's house at the edge of Houston's Third Ward. Though somewhat homey, the house also strongly reflected its main open-to-public intent with sharp spotlights focusing on masks or paintings, wide open rooms, and few sitting options. The hardwood floors throughout and pier-and-beam construction reminded me instantly of my old house.

Striking up a conversation with the owner, a former journalist, I noticed how he asked me questions. Today, aware of the dangers in turning a conversation into an all-about-me barrage of information, I attempted to steer the conversation back towards him. How did he come to find this house? How did he become interested in African art? Why did he choose to place a gallery here?

What I found was an interesting, well-travelled person willing to share his art, his space, and his knowledge with others. We also found something in common – a love of both art and older houses.

When engaging in a conversation with strangers, keep the focus on the other person. It makes you comfortable, puts them at ease, and might introduce you to a new friend.

NOTE #36

CHECK OUT ANTIQUE STORES

U ntil I lived in a small town, I never really paid much attention to antique shops and thrift stores. But, within the first year of arriving in small town life, that changed. There weren't exactly a lot of great art exhibits, concerts or plays locally. For entertainment, I traveled to the local antique shops.

The selections were enormous and varied. Want green glass? Red glass? How about an old desk with leather writing top? A framed photo of John Wayne? A coffee table?

I'm not saying I ever had the eye to find a good piece of furniture, a lamp or anything like that, but I always loved going to just look. Together with friends we would go visit antique shops all over town, and, without having to spend a whole lot of money, I furnished my house with bookcases, dressers, artwork, and glassware.

It also gave me a good, free-if-I-chose activity on the weekends.

After moving back to Houston in 2015, things in the antique arena really took a turn. My husband, with an exceptional eye, developed favorite places. We bought collections of old plates, each with a story, to go on the walls. We found old works of art, medieval-looking paintings on wood, Asian cabinets, glittering old crystal-shaded lamps, African masks, and more. We collected tapestries: some with French writing, some with old English. Some went on walls in the front room, some in the back, others went on the ceiling. People marveled when they came over, and each item evoked a story about where we found it. I could share with them about one-of-a-kind chairs that we had received, or the couch that arrived when I rented a box truck and drove underneath the Houston Galleria mall to pick it up, while successfully navigating the loading dock.

Antiques are easy to find, but good antiques require looking for items that stand out. Usually, they have a story. Who owned this treasure before me? What kind of life did it have? In some cases, I've had to fix furniture, or rewire lamps to get them to work safely. Each piece, whether it be because of an adventure to get it, or because of a story behind it, is unique. It's quirky, and it's ours.

Evan Vicchy's *5 Reasons Why People Buy Antiques* tells us that "for collectors, there is always a story as to why acquiring these objects is so meaningful to them."

Often, the reasons why antique collectors buy used items comes down in the following:

1. It connects us with the past.

Whether it's a vintage poster of an old movie, used books, or something from the Ming dynasty, people buy antiques because they're old. Holding a relic created before you were born connects us to different times.

2. It may be worth some money.

Not all antiques are worth something. When Michael and I find a trove of books, we like to go through and see what they're worth, but we never have intentions of selling them. Dealers like to acquire items and resell them for a profit, but most of us aren't destined to be dealers; we just get items for fun.

3. It represents time spent with someone.

Antiquing is an art that is best shared. Most pieces I buy at second-hand stores involves spending an afternoon with a friend or my spouse. Sometimes the antique acts as a reminder of that time.

4. The great chase for something eye-catching is addictive.

When I came upon the red Moroccan lamp, my eyes were immediately drawn to it. Its sleek, stained-glass pattern cast a reddish tinge on the table, and yet the shapes of the mosaic tiles made that reddish tinge seem to dance. Though I wasn't looking for a glass lamp, I knew it was a good find at a great price. It was unique and original.

5. It's an inexpensive way to spend time together.

The eclectic range of items in an antique store can spur great conversations. It also may lead to visits to different parts of towns, or even different parts of the state that we never saw before.

Last summer, after hearing about an authentic African mask, Michael and I piled the dogs in a rental car and drove four hours across Texas to the town of Brady, where we looked at a collection of masks once owned by Texas pediatrician and beloved Austinite Ben White.

With so much "new" in stores, it's nice to be able to decorate the house with old items that stand out. When I play the piano in the front room, I'm surrounded by old books, decorative lamps, art, and tapestries that provide an original uniqueness to our home.

When Michael and I got married, we held our reception at the house. During that lovely evening, we each told stories about the various items on the walls. The house itself became a conversation starter; something we were able to share with others. Shouldn't that be the importance of furniture anyway? Shouldn't the things in a home help propel the narrative of a collective life together? Antiques make a home unique and provide all sorts of shared experiences that bind us together.

NOTE #37

TAKE YOUR ULTIMATE OPINION

Sometimes it bothers me if people don't like me. "People pleasing," they call it. It's such a polite word. It doesn't really mean anything. It's kind of cute.

Through the help of others, I learned that this cute little character flaw, where I bend my life to someone who doesn't like me destroys me spiritually. Instead, I quit standing up because I don't want to hurt other people's feelings.

Not everyone is going to like me. Not everyone will think my comments are funny or my ideas witty. Some people just don't like one of my character traits.

We all have people who hate us – exes, workmates, people on the road, or whatever. It may be parents or children. It may be our current spouse or a former friend. It may be someone who we hope will forgive us but hasn't yet.

When I forgive someone, I no longer resent them. It may mean that I allow them back into my life, or it may mean that I just simply am not going to keep thinking about them. In the end, our job is not to worry about what they think of us. At some point, this may mean not attempting to right former wrongs anymore. It may mean letting someone go.

People pleasers often go out of their way for others' approval, even if it means using their own resources. They do it because of insecurities and lack of self-esteem. It's an addiction to validation.

They receive validation from others' opinions, and sometimes they give with the goal of being liked. They struggle trying to discuss hurt feelings and justify the other person's actions.

Long ago I was in a class where the professor was angry with me for not following his directions exactly. Though I am one who learns best experientially, I was chastised for not following his exact method in rehearsal.

"You're here to study with the master of this craft," he said, "and I am the master of your craft."

This man intimidated me, not in a manner of professional respect, but in a constant fear of attack. I ran my rehearsals in the manner I was told. I tried harder to please this professor, but nothing worked.

171

Eventually I finished that degree, we parted ways, and I began studying with a professor whom I respect and still hope to not disappoint.

My best teachers were the ones who sent me out to explore, fail, and then return and ask them why my method didn't work. Thank God there were more of them in store for me soon after that experience.

That intimidating experience taught me something else, too. It taught me that sometimes people hate you – even people who are influential over you. As time went on, I realized he tried his best, and that as a student I'm not the easiest to work with. Fortunately, many other professors at that school nurtured and encouraged me to continue my education.

I am also incredibly grateful for that man. He taught me how to ignore the people who don't like me. It's not pleasant or easy, and often takes a great deal of skill to "turn the other cheek," but I grew stronger after experiencing it.

When someone bothers me, the problem is never them. If what they say isn't true, I can ignore them, because they're ignorant to the situation, they made something up, or simply don't understand. When I get upset, it's because there's some hidden level of truth, worry, or idea that their opinion matters more than my own opinion about myself.

Is their opinion that important? What if they hate what I do?

This is where faith comes in. If I'm truly meant to be somewhere, God will put me there.   Here's what I learned: what others think of me *is none of my business.*

There are a few people whose opinion of me matters today: my family, a few close friends, and God. Everyone else I decide if their suggestion is helpful – and ignore them if it isn't.

NOTE #38

DEAL WITH DIFFICULT PEOPLE

When I was a music professor, it was painfully obvious to me that some people thought my position was useless. One of the sharpest examples came one winter night when I needed to leave early that evening because I had scholarship auditions in the morning.

"You mean you actually give *scholarships?*" this guy blurted out. "For people just to sing in *choir?!*" I turned around and walked away.

I wanted to tell him that choir connects students to one another. I wanted to tell him that the fine arts increase student retention and especially music, where we all work together to create something meaningful. Instead, I decided it wasn't worth it.

Most people don't intentionally try to hurt, and if they do, it may not cross their mind. When I'm disturbed about something that someone did "to me," usually the answer is that they're just doing something. The fact that I got hurt was a side effect. Unless it's bodily injury, it only hurt me because I allowed it to hurt.

I'm not saying I have an impenetrable emotional shield. Sometimes it would be wonderful if I did. Instead, I rehash that hurtful conversation, inserting new, wittier comebacks. I might even go so far as to share those comebacks with another person.

It's usually at that point that the anger for them lifts; it's silly. If the music I pick is not their favorite this week, or my writing fails to meet their expectations, it's ok. It's just one person's opinion.

Difficult people are often in our lives to teach us tolerance. If I don't like someone, I can do several things:

1. Accept others.

Not everyone is meant to get along with everyone else. Sometimes it's better to just get along with some and be accepting of the rest.

2. Tolerate the unlikeable.

It's good to have people with different viewpoints and mindsets. After all, being able to see the same problem from different angles makes a team stronger.

3. *Treat others with civility.*

One trait I have learned from my husband is the "stoic nod." With no expression at all, no acknowledgement, and no words, he shows that he heard whatever someone has said and doesn't react. This stops the other person's drama.

4. *Manage expectations.*

Does someone constantly talk down? Are they always criticizing my work? In a public situation, do they never acknowledge me, like I don't exist? People follow patterns, and if I am aware of their patterns and can predict them, I know that they are just being "normal."

5. *Focus on oneself.*

That negative colleague? The one that talks too much? The one that shouts all the time? Maybe I need to review my own positivity, talkativeness, or decibel level first.

6. *Pause.*

If someone has said something injurious, did I lash out at them, or did I take a moment to construct a better answer? Did I allow my response to be sarcastic and mean? Did I give a non-answer, a dead-pan face, and leave it at that?

7.   *Tell others what's needed.*

When all else fails, did I communicate to the other person the way I feel?   This is hard, especially if I'm people-pleasing.

8.   *Allow space.*

Can I walk away?   Can I see the other person with empathy?

I no longer carry the energy anymore to stay upset for long periods of time.   This is called allowing people to rent space in your head.   It made me unapproachable because someone might think I'll get mad.

That doesn't mean I don't get mad ever.   I just get mad a whole lot less, and never in front of the choir.   In fact, I have discovered a far more powerful tool in my arsenal: the truth.

In rehearsal, sometimes the choir can get rowdy. Most of the time this lasts only for a few minutes, and we get back to work.   Sometimes it gets out of hand. Once in the last few years it *really* got out of hand, but instead of getting angry, I told the truth.

"Guys, we're spending too much time laughing and not enough time singing."

I lowered my voice a bit while I said this, so I sounded serious.   Immediately, the choir got serious too.   The choir wasn't out to get me or get even for making them rehearse!   They were just acting silly that night, and just by asking, the result was loving, understanding, and a renewed focus.

Every job, every situation contains difficult people. Our job is to accept them where they are, practice self-care to keep them from bothering us, and state the truth if they hurt us. We owe it to ourselves to make the best effort to get along without getting injured.

NOTE #39

YOUR FEELINGS ARE IRRELEVANT

A bout once a month I sift through the church videos, making sure they are noted in the music licensing website. In today's world, all music online must be reported to a licensing agency. As a result, I report it at various intervals.

I hate this part of my job. It's repetitive and dull. It's not conducting choirs or preparing rehearsals. I don't get to plan for it by sitting at the piano. I don't develop strategies to teach, extend vocal ranges, or remember rhythms.

When I sit down to report the music, I confront the thought that I really don't want to be doing this. I look for any excuse to do something else. I'll file music! I'll mop the floor! I'll do anything but make the song report.

In the end, I get started, plucking away at each video. I open YouTube with the monitor on the left, scanning the title and copyright information and type it in my document on the right. Later, I take that document and upload each song into the licensing website.

The time I need to do this seemingly herculean task seems endless, but once I start takes extraordinarily little time; usually less than an hour or two per month. In fact, the hardest part of the ordeal is just sitting down.

I feel this way about a lot of things I don't really want to do. I don't want to jog in the subdivision. I don't want to mow the lawn. I don't want to get up early on Sundays.

There are mornings when I wake up and I don't want to do anything! I'd rather just lay in bed, but my back hurts and my mind starts on a tear about what I should do today, and I'm up. If I ignore this voice, I do the task in front of me and wonder why I ever thought about rejecting it.

Routines carry their own compulsion. Several years ago, I started writing down prayers every day. I was regular and disciplined about this, and I thought that at some point I would even share it with others; maybe even publish it. Then the flood happened, and my work turned upside down. I quit writing the daily prayers.

This is caused by procrastination and has several reasons. Sometimes I tell myself that I'm "using my time more effectively," instead of calling it what it is.

Next, I need to evaluate the task. Is it overwhelming, unpleasant, or could it lead to more work? Can I create a to-do list, and stick to a plan?

One morning I had no desire to run. I stepped out the door. *I don't want to do this. It's not for me.* I thought to myself.

I closed the garage door, thinking how much I hate this. What if it rains? It might be too muggy and too hot. My head hurts a little tiny bit. I didn't sleep well. I got to the end of the street, where I call the "run point," and started running. Now, bouncing with each step came the firm "no," both from my mind and now my body. There were cars, and I swear the kid with the backpack walked to the bus stop faster than I ran.

Still, I continue. After all, some of these houses have some great yards. What kind of trees are those? How do they keep their grass looking so good? That house looks just like ours, but with grey stucco on the front and a paver-lined walkway to the backyard. What a lovely life they must lead!

Now I've rounded the first and second corners, and even though my shoes have untied, I know with just a little more push I will run further than I have since I started this process.

Rehearsal can be like that too. We come up, excited for the music, but dreading the masks, the "social distancing," the not being able to share music, or not being able to hear one another. We clamor, trying to get the air and articulation we need.

Just like the houses and yards on my running journey, we start passing notes and sections that we love. We sigh as they go by, wrapped in the beauty of the chords and the otherworldliness of singing and music making. For a moment, the masks, or the face shield - which, for the record, I hate - aren't so bad; they're a small price with a big payoff.

One author I read this summer says to use the phrase "get to."

I get to see you.
I get to make music with you.
I get to direct - even though it's been a while.
I get to sing along.
I get to come here to this lovely, air-conditioned place, and never once have to spray for wasps.
And I get to watch you grow and develop as singers - now for the second time.

Changing the inner narrative stops procrastination. Instead of acting like I'm forced to do a task, say I "get to" do that task. Also, I bargain with myself – do the task and receive a reward, or don't do it and keep dreading it.

Another little trick is to carve out a specific time for that task. My best computer work is done on days where there are no rehearsals. Setting up a routine has helped stop procrastination.

My wants eventually evolve into what *needs* to be done, and in fact, I wonder why I ever thought that I didn't want to do something in the first place. In other words: *my feelings don't matter*.

I found that if I just show up and try, the work gets done, whether I wanted to do it or not, and my feelings follow suit.

NOTE #40

PUT YOUR PHONE DOWN

Weaving through a series of canyons, Texas FM 170 is not for the faint of heart. First, it ascends and descends with gut wrenching drops worthy of a propeller plane in a thunderstorm. It moves sharply to the left and right, sometimes following a very muddy, fast-moving Rio Grande, and other times through rugged, craggy mountains. It ascends high over passes complete with stone-fashioned walls to keep the occasional distracted driver from careening to his death.

I was curious about this route. It used to be a smuggler's road, and at one point the road even crosses "Banditos (Robber's) Canyon." This series of Spanish roads earned the ominous name "Death of the Burro," because of the tremendous mountain pass about 15 miles outside of Lajitas, Texas.

The Rio Grande moves quickly through this part of the desert and is a milky-whitish, mud-laden river. After the rains fell the night before, it was easy to see why it could carve out vast canyons through the foreboding rocks that overlook its banks.

This is a part of Texas that's isolated and remote. It's not on the way to somewhere else; it is a destination. Outside the confines of my rental car, I'm confronted by another deafening roar: the roar of total and absolute silence.

It's all around me, along with the cliffs, shrubs, and rocks. The silence is complete. I stop to take another video. And another. And another. Each time, I'm rewarded by the absence of sound. The engine is off and other than a gentle breeze, there is nothing. No birds, crickets, cars, people, traffic, radios, or anything to disturb it.

It is the ultimate "social distancing."

Though my time in Big Bend Ranch State Park was not long enough and was cut even shorter by the dirt roads washing out, it was an extraordinary experience. I see why my grandparents kept packing up a travel trailer and heading to this desolate area year after year.

Perhaps the best part of this trip was the eerie music that accompanied it on the radio. First came Claude Debussy's *Nocturnes*, a study in the shades of color of the orchestra. The haunting pattern by the oboe and the parallelism in the strings accompany this raw chasm between two countries, an eerie, un-earthly place, far removed from the freeways and byways of mega-cities like Houston.

Topping the Parisian otherworldliness of Debussy's *Nocturnes,* Stravinsky's *Firebird* suite begins playing, written around the same time, in the same city. As I drove with no cell phone signal in sight for miles, I couldn't help but let my mind wander and my spirit soar with the mountains. Who needs YouTube videos when you've got all this?

It is estimated that Americans spend more than 5 hours a day looking at our phones. Younger adults spend almost 6 – that's a fourth of our day! There are no pauses; nothing to appreciate. I, too, spend a large amount of time looking at email, YouTube, reading news articles, and playing solitaire when I'm standing in line.

Some authors call this "the addiction" of our phones. In zoom meetings, even talking with friends, I find myself sometimes slipping into the "clean up the email" mantra. In fact, after coming back to my room after a full day in Big Bend Ranch State Park, my first thought was to go to my email and "clear it out." What items needed to be addressed? What can be ignored? Being a crafty conductor, I follow the advice I heard: label things as "imminent," "important," or "non-essential."

The problem I keep having is that the "important" keeps slipping into "imminent," and the "non-essential" into "important." Today, several emails came in from church. I could have ignored them; after all, I'm on vacation for the first time in a year. Hyper-connectivity means that sometimes it's essential for me to get my opinions out. My ideas matter.

This is one of the main reasons I love flying so much. For an hour or two, a door is shut, and I am unreachable – the phone is off. The rules are made for me; I don't have to make up excuses or wonder why I haven't received an email or checked the weather in the last fifteen minutes. I'm free to walk around the cabin, turbulence permitting, free to talk to others in my row, or not. I'm free to read my book. I'm free to look outside and marvel – something I only get to do on the ground in large national parks.

So, I'm writing this not as much for you as for me. Joel, put your phone down.

NOTE #41

USE AN ALARM CLOCK

Recently a couple of girls from church sent me graduation invitations. One was going to attend my alma mater, one going to my sister's alma mater. I got them a few items for new dorm rooms, but one thing I sent to both girls was an alarm clock.

I'm amazed at how many people don't use alarm clocks! When I taught college, typically I taught the early classes at 8AM, and I did this for two reasons. First, because I found that after a ton of coffee I am at my brightest, freshest, and funniest – all essential to teaching. Second, I was not conflicting with other classes or private lessons, which might take away some of the students that needed to take my class. The brightest and best seemed motivated to come to early morning classes, and those who were not as motivated eventually stopped coming.

Though I loved teaching morning classes, I hated getting up at the crack of dawn and especially trudging into the office before first light. The semesters I taught classes at 7AM were tough, but the moment I saw those students I felt energized by the exciting material – sight singing.

In those days, I had a black and white border collie named Poog. With a voracious appetite and an equally high energy level, he lived for routines that involved long walks starting no later than 5 AM. Usually, around 4:30, he jumped on the bed and started whimpering. By 5, I gave up. Some mornings I let him out in the backyard, but most of the time we walked through the neighborhood, and immediately came back for a delicious breakfast of grain-free kibble.

Though Poog normally acted as the alarm, the alarm clock set Poog off too. It's gentle beeping meant one thing – breakfast was approaching. Poog got excited, started wagging his tail, walking up to the side of the bed, and whining at me until I opened my eyes. If I needed to wake up early, that alarm would go off, calling Poog to arms that a new breakfast was on the horizon.

As a result of an alarm clock and a dog, I am never late for morning classes, early morning services, or any other morning time. As a professor, I always appreciated when my students were on time for class. As a music director, I still appreciate those who show up at 7AM on Sunday mornings, methodically putting out the coffee and other items so that church members can klatch in the activity room.

This small but dedicated group of people consistently glide in, Sunday after Sunday, armed with donuts, creamers, coffee urns, and whatever food they see fit to bring. They're not part of our staff; they don't have anyone overlooking them, they just do it.

They probably use alarm clocks. One day I asked them. They all do. One uses his phone alarm, but I'm sure, being an engineer, he's meticulous about charging that phone every night.

In centuries past, people used all kinds of methods for wake-up calls. Church bells, door knockers and rudimentary alarms gave rise to mechanical clocks. Since the late 19th century, the wind-up alarm clock became standard, and later the electric alarm clock. As society became more ritualized with job start-times, (thanks to the rise of industry, factories, and retail) precise wake-up times became more important. Today, alarm clocks of all types are a staple of most bedrooms - until recently.

Over the last ten to fifteen years a new trend developed: the phone alarm. Some apps mimic alarm clocks by using large digital displays. Other apps are built in, simply coming on at the appropriate time with a gentle or harsh sound.

As years went by, teaching my early classes, I noticed that the students who used phones had more trouble coming to class because they would either forget to reset the alarm, or the phone might run out of power during the night. Having a consistent device just for waking up means that the device can be reset and turned back "on" immediately after waking up.

Though Poog has long since gone, I still have two dogs who continue the tradition of waking me around 5AM. Every day – weekends included – I wake just before dawn to greet my dogs, feed them, and, on Saturday mornings, do what I did as a kid.

I go back to sleep.

Note #42

Learn to Praise and Deflect

In the movie *Hancock*, Will Smith, playing the post-modern superhero, is told he must bolster the feelings of others. During a violent shootout in downtown Los Angeles, he flies onto the building, with bullets raining around him.

Hancock stops in his tracks and looks at one member of the SWAT team.

"Oh yeah. Good job."

He turns to the other SWAT members:

"Good job."

The policemen say nothing as he lifts himself awkwardly off the building towards the shootout.

The strangeness on both sides is funny. Attempting his new skill, his inopportune congratulations catch the others by surprise.

While we can't identify with flying without a plane or being impervious to bullets, many of us can certainly identify with unpleasant circumstances or an awkward "good job."

I assumed awkwardness and shyness were some romantic notions of being a misunderstood artist, but as time passed, I realized this is a normal part of humanity.

"Good job's" don't always mean what we think they should. "Why You Should Stop Saying 'Good Job' and What to Say Instead," from *The Pragmatic Parent,* warns that blanket "good job's" offer little substance and create insincere praise. Instead, the article offers, try specific words.

When I was learning to teach elementary, I learned to focus on a student who was exhibiting appropriate behavior by saying:

> *"I really like the way _____ is sitting quietly."*

> *"Thank you for not playing the instrument until you're told to."*

The word "you" plays prominently in these types of praise so that they seem both sincere and genuine. In the movie, Will Smith's generic "good job," and his deadpan delivery reeks both of insincerity and awkwardness because of the generic nature of the compliment.

However, it's important, especially in a group situation, to not make the problem-solving all about the members of the group. In other words, watch how much to use the word "you."

When I was first learning to conduct, I tended to over-praise. In reality, I was just glad that the ensemble members were following my directing. One day, I was asked about my language in rehearsal by my friend Mark. "Have you ever thought about just talking about the music, and not about *us?*"

I didn't understand. How does one *not* talk about the people in the ensemble? My directions usually centered around saying things like, "You sang too choppy." "You didn't sing that note right," or "Can you be softer there?"

Inexperienced conductors, I've noticed, still do this just as I did.

My friend explained that instead of focusing on the people, to focus on the *task* – the music. Instead of saying "you sang it choppy," say "the music calls for smooth there." Instead of "you sang that wrong," try "lets review the notes." Instead of "can you be softer," try "the music says *piano* (soft)." I can even make fun of the music, saying "Altos, why was the composer so *mean* to you there." (I use this one a lot, because the altos typically get the hard notes.)

Correcting people repeatedly hurts their feelings and their morale. Instead, I show how the problem is actually in the music. I call this "deflection." This has the effect of taking the problem and removing it from a personal context. "Of course you missed that note! If that composer was in *my* class, I would have failed him for writing such a horrible line!"

After they get the problem right, then I can say "good job." Since we have focused on one particular area and they knew the problem had been fixed, they deserve a little praise!

Praise and deflection can be a delicate balance when working with others. On the one hand, we want our co-workers or teams to get better. On the other hand, we want them to remain excited to be a part of our team.

So, for those that master this skill, good job.

NOTE #43

ACCEPT ERRORS BEFORE
OVERCOMING THEM

Directing choirs means standing in front of others and potentially telling them how to sing. I know that the number one fear of most choristers is that the director will single them out for being terrible singers, especially in the middle of rehearsal.

In singing, we use our bodies, and attach our sense of self-worth to that singing. Calling a singer out, telling them they sound awful, or their voices are bad is akin to saying their personality stinks or their children are ugly.

Absolute honesty without compassion is brutality. It has no place in the rehearsal room, the board room, or the online platform.

When I coach amateur singers, I tend to follow the following guidelines:

1. *The problem is about... the problem.*

Tuning problems? Vowel matching? Wrong notes? Incorrect rhythm? Late to rehearsal? Those problems are specific and do not involve criticizing the person. Make it about the problem.

This also works away from the rehearsal room. Is the other person making errors in their work? Is the final product not up to standards? Where, specifically, is the problem?

2. *Define the solution.*

Sometimes people don't follow because they don't know how! With my singers, I diagnose and identify the answer. Tuning problems are usually caused by poor vowels. Wrong notes are usually because they haven't been taught well. Tardiness may require more flexibility on my part, or a simple request.

Maybe the technique was learned incorrectly. Maybe the other person is just having an off day. Either way, I need to articulate a solution.

3. *Be upfront.*

When I was in college, I worked at a company in the mall that sold video tapes. It was a part-time "temp" job for Christmas, and I joined for the holiday rush. During that month, I didn't always know what I was doing. The manager constantly looked at me, relayed a message to one of the other cashiers, and he would then come up to me and correct the latest infraction.

That manager couldn't seem to be bothered with a brand-new, temporary employee. When the holiday ended, I was glad to never set foot in that store again.

The lesson is clear. If there's a problem, be direct. Usually, it clears up fast.

4. Don't get emotional.

As a young director, I blew up at students who acted silly or didn't pay attention during rehearsal. If they weren't giving their all, I would blast them. That was awful; especially because I carried that anger long after rehearsal.

One day watching the revised *Battlestar Galactica* on TV, I heard something the lead character said.

"DON'T GET EMOTIONAL! Work the problems."

It was a sudden and transformative revelation about my own work with others. For years, I let my emotions rule me.

When the problems happened in rehearsal, my thought process was:

1. The situation was bad.
2. I didn't teach it right.
3. I screwed it up.
4. I can't get them to do it correctly.
5. It'll never get better.

not in the traditional dark and damp sense. It was bone dry, tall, and yet not foreboding. Occasionally I heard other explorers' laughter as they talked to one another. I made videos and took photos, channeling my inner YouTube hero.

Watching all those YouTube travel videos gave me the courage to experience some of those places myself. Though I didn't camp, I climbed, explored, and dreamed.

So often, those of us who live in cities and towns don't go looking for nature. We're content to visit other cities and go to shows and movies. We buy shirts that boast of places. We gather antiques and kitschy mementos. We visit friends and Instagram-able locales tagging it "best day ever."

In traveling into nature, I learn about the world around me, but I also learn more about myself. How is my meditation and prayer practice? How aware am I of my surroundings? How is my sense of peace? Without the distractions of others, can I feel closer to God?

Each time I visit nature, I get to reassess my spiritual development in these areas while discovering some of the jewels of this planet. Perhaps the times that I am most authentic to myself are those trips where I have the freedom to drive anywhere, see anything, and enjoy the companionship of good books, myself, and my God.

NOTE #45

FIND YOUR PURPOSE

Maybe it's the years of graduate school where my assignments and my conducting were regularly evaluated and judged. When I post YouTube videos, I turn off the comments. I don't leave reviews. I shy away from talking about my opinions unless asked.

For years, my opinions about my own abilities, my thoughts, even my writing skills, led me to the darkest places. "If you only knew me," I thought, until I found out that such thoughts are egomania and self-centeredness. My own pride pushed out my creativity. Writing? Let's play the old tape from that professor. Conducting? How about the time that I got passed over for that opportunity? Teaching? What about the dozens of jobs I applied for and never got?

When I constantly judge myself to be *too lousy,* I negate my opportunity to be helpful. Maybe I'm not the best singer, best piano player, best conductor, best writer, best musician. Who cares? If I don't do it, it doesn't happen. What if I'm *exactly how I am supposed to be*? What if God made me as I was needed?

When I was jobless, sleeping on a couch, and looking for a change, I was afraid. The career path I thought was mine for the taking was gone. It was only at this point that I started earnestly doing what others had asked of me for *years* – I started to pray every day.

"God – put me where you need me most."

I let go and began applying to other jobs. I took temporary work, fixing houses with my hands and my growing army of tools. I wrote, I prayed more, and I thought about it. I asked for my purpose.

Then one day the answer came – slowly, gently: I was being prepared for another job, one that would lead me to a happier existence. I finally put the academic life away and found something better. I lead others in choral music today from where they are, not where they need to be based on learning outcomes. Today's objective is to believe in others so that they will overcome their own singing fears and give glory to their Creator by doing their best.

How do we discover our purpose?

1. Do an inventory. Find what you're good at.

Are you a good painter? Talker? Baker? Do you like crafts? Are you good with your hands? Do you enjoy cars? People? Write it down.

Also, write down what you'd *like* to be good at. Not all of us are imbued with talents from birth, despite what some would have you believe. Some of us must work for our abilities – hard.

2. Ask yourself: "If I could do the same thing every day, what would it be?"

The important idea here is not to capture the perfect job or employer but find out what skills you would like to use. In my case, I like to talk, write, pray, conduct, encourage others, make music, and work with my hands.

3. Whose opinions matter to you? What do they think?

Each of us requires feedback. One friend kept telling me, "God didn't bring you this far to drop you off."

When I changed careers, the people I respected the most were encouraging without meddling; enthusiastic but not unrealistic, and great soundboards to help me steer through uncertainty.

4. What if you're wrong?

There are *no* wrong decisions! Investigate. Look around. God gives us lots of opportunities to make our presence known. Rarely, even in the worst mistake, does that decision end without new knowledge, confidence, or security.

Even the worst job may cause us to re-evaluate something in our lives or give us doubt. A venture, however futile it seems, never leaves us lacking in new information, even if that information is "I shouldn't do this."

5. Ask God.

Having a modicum of faith helps in this aspect. I believe that the universe never makes mistakes. We each have a place and a purpose. Think about it: every decision you've made to this point – including whether to pick up this book – has brought you to these exact words, at this specific time.

Someone once said, "On what slender threads our destiny hangs."   Why not ask God, the architect of all this, to help make those decisions? Perhaps the path for us is laid out all along, right in front of us. We find our purpose by making those decisions.

Don't make decisions in fear. Make them in faith.

NOTE #46

GO PROVE IT

Toxic shame stunted my growth.

I imagined that, as I wrote, former professors would sit in the lounge making jokes and quips about my questionable intelligence, language skills, and suspect musical ability.

When I finished my doctoral project, I felt that I had been awarded the degree by mistake. When it was over, I was sure I'd feel some sort of pride about finishing, but instead all I felt was relief, shame, and exhaustion. It would be more than ten years before I would write again.

Why do we allow flawed ideas to have power over us, especially toxic ones?

Sometimes we allow others' comments to internalize as cold, fast truths. It took time to take that power away and return it back to me. In the meantime, I sought out friends – people whom I hand selected for their input. I wrote pages for them, and they sent me feedback. They asked how my writing was going. They sent encouragement.

In one case, my friend Anne saw my slow struggle, and as my own dam of creativity broke, I saw hers do the same, and she started working on her own book. In a moment of great pride for me, she asked me to review her work, as much as in the same way I asked her to review mine almost a year earlier.

As though a floodgate opened, I started writing one day. With the help of Anne and other friends, I found my own voice and my own way to fight back from the monsters of the past that had metastasized in my head. I watched those fears melt away to the nothingness from which they came.

Out of that came a second emotion: regret. I allowed naysayers to dictate what I could and couldn't do for years. I allowed someone's negative ideas to impact my waking thoughts, my emotions, and to stop my progress.

Releasing that shame and guilt was difficult. It took time. I started reviewing my own writing habits. Most of all, I found friends who continued to encourage and support me through my writing. They celebrated with the successes, and they waded faithfully through the failures.

Other things began happening once I released this shame too. I began playing the piano more often and enjoying it. During the pandemic, I started playing from a book of Bach sonatas and little fugues that I had put aside for more than a decade. From this, almost daily I sit and play. It's never perfect, but it's enjoyable. Someday I'll record it for church – or not. It's mine to decide. I began composing small pieces for the services during lockdown, no longer worried if someone would write about how it isn't "good enough," or "masterful."

Meditation, self-compassion, and forgiveness help overcome the toxicity of shame. Sadly, we sometimes go through our lives accepting what someone said to us as sacrosanct. It is as much reality as our hair and eye color.

Sometimes toxic shame influences whether we like something or not. After all, if I've accepted the idea that I *can't* do something, I'm far less likely to enjoy it. Here are some common forms of toxic shame:

- I can't cook. (Cooking takes practice.)
- I can't do math. (Again, math requires practice.)
- I can't sing. (Most people can; only a select few have physiological vocal problems inhibiting them from matching pitch.)
- I can't speak in front of crowds. (Most of us feel anxiety at this. The trick is managing the anxiety and accepting that it comes.)

There's no such thing as a committee that identifies our lacking abilities and stamps us as "can't." We create these parameters around ourselves.

Stop it.

Take the first step into the unknown. Enjoy the drawing class with friends. Sign up for the pottery course or the community chorus. The longer "can't" exists, the more barriers exist between you and the good you bring to others.

At the end of the day, we all have abilities inside each of us that are not perfect: playing softball, organization, working out, teaching, speaking, and yes, even writing. Before ignoring those abilities, don't shut down because someone a long time ago told you how you'd never be able to do it. Tell them their opinion of you doesn't matter. Then go prove it.

NOTE #47

GET A CHEERLEADING SQUAD

"Why the hell he's still there, I don't know," Shirey mumbled to his University Christian Church choir in 2006. I had come down to visit him, and he invited me to join his beloved church choir for rehearsal that night.

At the time, Shirey had been hinting at the idea that I should move up in my career and find something different. At that time in my life, I wasn't interested in leaving my small town.

Shirey, the curmudgeon of a university professor and church choir director had a rather forceful way of eliciting sound out of the choir. He'd nitpick, cajole, sometimes yell, and often work with great intensity. The two things that Shirey did with tremendous success: directed a choir – especially in music of the Renaissance – and support his former students.

From 1976 until his death in 2009, Mr. Shirey was the choral director at Texas Christian University in Fort Worth and was my college conducting professor. He could be tough, mean, and tenacious, but he was always upfront.

What wasn't expected were the things that he did behind the scenes. One summer our choir was invited to sing at the Dallas convention of the American Guild of Organists. Since I lived in Houston, I stayed overnight with a couple at the local Disciples of Christ church.

"Mr. Shirey speaks very highly of you," my host said as I got out of the car. I was kind of shocked. I didn't think he really paid a lot of attention to me. Later I would come to understand something about my choir director: he pushed his students hard and bragged about us. I suddenly realized what a treasure he really was in my life. He still pushed me. He still made me mad, but he was in my corner.

Shirey had been, for better or worse, my cheerleader. (Maybe it would be better to call him a yell-leader.) He was always pushing me to move up the academic ladder; to find a better position. The day of his funeral, with dozens of choristers around me, I understood St. Augustine's phrase, "He who sings prays twice."

My family and friends also cheer my accomplishments, mourn the losses, and console me in the defeats. Some friends encourage me to write, to

213

compose music, and respond with love, compassion, and honesty to my ideas. They tell me, "Yes, you can do these things," and if it's not a good idea, they gently discourage me.

None of us gets through this world truly alone. We all have people who we work with or for, people who we live with, people who we discuss plans with, and people who we have business transactions with. Not all of them are nice, but among them all are people who care enough about each of us to want us to succeed. They rejoice just as much in our successes as they do in their own, because they get to have a part in our successes too.

Cathy Caprino, senior writer for Forbes Magazine, says, "These inspirers have grown comfortable being totally authentic and open about who they really are deep down (warts and all). They no longer worry that they'll be rejected, scorned and put down."

When I first started to let others in, allowing them to know more about the "real" me, I worried about how, especially as a conductor, they would relate if I was imperfect; if I didn't know what I was doing most times. I put forth a façade and tried and persuade others that I had a reason for everything I did.

I didn't like that person.

When I started watching others who seemed comfortable with themselves, what I noticed most – what I was drawn to – was the *authenticity*. One authentic woman I knew spoke of her anger at her ex-husband; one man talked of his flashbacks to Vietnam; one woman talked of her desire to be a part of her daughter's life again.

These were not perfect people. They earned my respect because they had to overcome adversity and difficult lives, and they felt comfortable enough to talk about it. I heard speakers say things like "…but when I'm feeling insecure, I don't want to get up here and talk."

I told on myself more. I made fun of my insecurities and told others about them. During rehearsal, I teased about my inabilities.

The funniest thing happened: I became *relatable.* How many of us never have a bad day or wonder what someone else is doing? How many of us have personality flaws and issues that we must admit? It seemed that the more flawed I am, the better my rehearsal goes!

Our inspirers show us about humility *because* they weren't super-people. They were real people with real flaws and issues. They made mistakes, had to forgive themselves, and had to move forward, just like I do.

Conductors, I was taught, needed to approach music from a place of vulnerability. How can I connect with the ensemble if I am not myself? How can I be vulnerable if I don't have a friend to share those vulnerabilities with?

215

So find a cheering section. They are the people who want what's best for you. They also may be the ones who look at your work with a critical eye in a loving manner. Let them cheer for you.

NOTE #48

WORK IN YOUR YARD

In late December, the trees in the back lose all their leaves, and in March, as spring is coming, the oak tree in front finally sheds its leaves.

Since December is leaf-blowing season, at Christmastime, I knew what I wanted: a powerful leaf blower. After receiving it, I put on my goggles, hearing protection, and mask – a must to stop the pollen and mold allergies. Starting in the back corner of the yard I aimed my newly purchased lawn device at the ground, turned the wheel to the lowest setting, and marveled at the speed with which the leaves moved. Little by little, my yard went from a brown pile of leaves back to a funky green from the winter grasses that grow in Southeast Texas.

This year was different, though. Now I had my new lawn device, capable of whipping up a tornado of cleansing at almost 200 miles per hour. In about 20 minutes, I had created a mountain. I removed the leaves from the nooks and crannies of the yard; between the shed and the fence, in the small chasm beyond the gate, and across the back.

In the dull buzz of the whirling tornado-device, my thoughts wander. In fact, every time I mow the lawn, the steady stream of noise, repetitive back-and-forth paths cut by the mower, and the fresh air combined with the hot sun allow my usually busy mind to cease. My creative brain takes over, sometimes reliving old memories, dreaming up new ideas for writing or new projects for the house, creating new ideas for the church, and deciding on rehearsal techniques or warm-ups. In short, it is a meditative state that is only possible when my conscious mind is busy.

In a way, cleaning the yard serves a similar purpose as walking the labyrinth. There is a pattern with the endpoint always in sight. As the work progresses, a change can be seen; chaotic grasses or leaves turn to orderly ritual. The blight of neglected growth can be transformed into a sea of common length.

It is a forced pause from my work, made possible by necessity, but also serving as an inspiration point. Though it would be far more efficient and easier to hire someone to do my yard for me, there's a sense of accomplishment and joy working through my own grass, sculpting it into a regular, neat pattern.

The paths inside my mind receive a cleansing too. Maybe there was a problem or emotional imbalance that I had been clinging to. Maybe there was a resentment that I hadn't asked God to remove. Maybe there was a new project that I didn't even think about, waiting to be unearthed.

Creating tangible patterns helps to restore harmony both in the earth around my house and the space in my mind. It focuses me, requires my full attention to be divorced from the telephone or email, and genuinely leads me into a peaceful path. At the end, I have accomplished something truly remarkable.

Psychology Today says that the repetitive action of mowing does enable a calmer state of mind. The lawn tool manufacturer Ryobi reminds readers that it allows us to know our yard well, heading off problems like brown patch or flooding.

Some say that mowing the yard might be the only time we get to walk around and truly admire our lawn, while accomplishing something at the same time. Plus, we view any potential problems the yard might hide.

The other day I mowed, edged, and blew the sidewalks clean with my fast blower. My lights shine a little brighter on the tree, the pollen is out of the way, and the cars don't track leaves into the garage. The dogs get to spend some much-needed time outside while I'm edging, and sometimes I even get to pet the neighbor's dog.

I keep up my own yard both for the sake of the yard and the sake of my soul. Some of my best thinking has come out of inspiration I received from mowing. Though I never look forward to it, I always enjoy it when I do. After all, doesn't having a palatial, green yard give a feeling of accomplishment?

It's a moment to pause and think. It's a moment to experience outside and nature. It's a moment to see how land and house and sky come together. In doing the yard, we get to connect with the earth that supports us and connects us all together.

NOTE #49

TAKE TIME FOR YOURSELF

In sixth grade, my English teacher made us memorize a poem each week. Though I have forgotten many of them, this one I remembered:

Take Time

Take time to think:
it is the source of power.

Take time to read;
it is the foundation of wisdom.

Take time to play;
it is the secret of staying young.

Take time to be quiet;

Singing in the Moment

it is the opportunity to see God.

Take time to be aware;
it is the opportunity to help others.

Take time to love and be loved;
it is God's greatest gift.

Take time to laugh;
it is the music of the soul.

Take time to be friendly;
it is the road to happiness.

Take time to dream;
it is what the future is made of.

Take time to pray;
it is the greatest power on earth.

Author Unknown

"No time" is the anthem for many of us enveloped in our busy-ness. In today's world, we get up, take care of our kids, our pets, our spouses, or our parents, grab something to eat, jump in the car, drive two hours listening to that favorite morning show, spend time at work, doing whatever "work-stuff" we do, then maybe go on to a second job to help make ends meet, often driving long distances there. We come home, exhausted, and wonder why we have nothing to say on the weekends.

Even God rested occasionally; weekly, in fact. When did we? In American culture, we celebrate our busyness. The main way to accomplish getting nice things, living in nice places, and having a great, comfortable life is to work hard. Then, one day the doctor's office calls and recommends more tests and just like that, our world changes.

Even Superman worked two jobs – newspaper reporter by day, superhero by night. Captain Kirk of *Star Trek* considered his starship as close to a spouse as he would ever get. Ellen Ripley from the *Alien* movies never could get away from the creatures that attach themselves to faces. In today's post-modern society, we would probably focus not on their heroic actions, but on the failed relationships that fell in their wakes. Is this true in "real life?" Did we stop taking time?

Like our fictional heroes, I love to be busy, too. I feel useful and needed – something we all aspire to. I imagine making big decisions and having people and things around me that need fixing, and of course they need my advice.

But sometimes I get tired of being useful, and I sometimes feel…used. When this happens, it is more important than ever that I recharge. In the past few years, I have made this recharging an excuse to rent a cabin, hole up, and write. Writing is not everyone's cup of tea, but I found it gave me a great deal of excitement to see the words arrive on the page, the pages to grow, and the book flesh out as time went on.

So far, my excursions led to places all over Texas: Galveston, Smithville, Marfa, Wimberley, and of course my little home office. Each place comes with a routine, perfect for pandemic writing or pre-pandemic writing. I write for a few hours in the morning, take a walk, then write until evening, take another walk, go to bed, and do it again.

This pattern gives me three benefits. First, it's predictable and doesn't cost a tremendous amount of money. Changing my surroundings immediately changes my mood and puts my thoughts in a totally different gear. Second, it allows me to visit different places I wouldn't otherwise go. This comes with perks. After a few days, I can "reward" myself with a trip to see some stores, or go into town, or even visit a state or national park nearby. Third, the trip itself – just the drive – becomes an inspiration, and though it's work, it seems more like fun than work, because I am experiencing a new place.

Taking time doesn't mean a far-away destination filled with exciting night life and fantastic cultural experiences. Sometimes it just means stepping away, doing something enjoyable, reconnecting with loved ones, and spending time with yourself.

Shortly after our church flooded in 2017, First Christian Church of Tulsa contacted me, anxious to see if we could use 300 hymnals. Our lower floor of the sanctuary seated over 450 people, each with a red Chalice Hymnal attached to the seatback in front. I never considered asking to have the boxes shipped. It was much more economical for me to get in my car and drive seven hours to Tulsa to get them.

Instead of taking the interstates – through Dallas, Oklahoma City and finally Tulsa, I chose to make a short-cut through the "pine curtain" of East Texas: Athens, Canton, Paris, Hugo, and finally up the long turnpike. Before I left, my husband begged me not to make the whole drive in a day. I said OK and took off, Tulsa bound. As the miles passed, I felt the weight of the intense clean-up work falling away. As the bright October day passed, I relaxed, feeling the usual rush as my little car whisked through the miles.

After hours of talk radio and electronic dance music, ten minutes in Tulsa collecting hymnals, and after heading back towards Houston, I knew I needed to stop. I pulled off the highway in the town of Hugo, Oklahoma, near the Texas border, and found a place to stay. With a Wal-Mart across the street and gas station close by, I found food, plenty to read, and a quick rest waiting in an unfamiliar town.

Arriving at the church the following day, I was re-energized after a road trip adventure not knowing where I would wind up. After being in "emergency clean-up" mode since the flood, the pause gave me the strength to move on with the daunting project that still lay ahead: re-assembling our choir program from multiple off-site locations back into our one campus.

Taking time for myself means just that – not rushing through everything in a hurry. It means waiting, going slowly, and taking the long road. It means enjoying the experience with a view to heighten the thrill of the journey.

NOTE #50

USE YOUR SHOES

Dust from reconstruction fills the air and covers me every time I go in. The dust covers everything. Dust from new concrete work; dust from sanded joint compound; dust from recent drilling; dust from millwork. Soon there will be dust from the stage, and dust from sanding down wood.

The creative process is messy. When fixing a building, it's dust and debris. It's large trash receptacles and piles of dirt. It's glue and sticky stuff and globs of paint.

I need to wear shoes right up until the point where the "old" becomes the new, then I know what I need to do. The shoes must come off, and the new, completed work needs to be trod barefoot, carefully with each step.

In writing, I write down and later re-write. It means re-exposing old stories. It's discovering areas of my life long forgotten. It's uncovering things I loved. The shoes go on until the rewrite, then the shoes come off, so I can feel the substance of the words.

In the world of music, creativity means analyzing new melodies. My shoes tromp through melodic contour, counterpoint, and countermelody. I identify where to use head voice versus chest voice or left versus right hand. It means calculating the apex of a phrase and determining which is the best diction. It means practicing something repeatedly until it's a part of my being. Then, it's shoes off and feel the composer's intent.

In graduate school, we had these awful things called "play and sings," where we sang one line of music while playing another; then while playing two lines. Not being a terribly proficient pianist, I hated "play and sing." It made more sense to me to sing the parts in my head.

Then I heard about choral conductor Robert Shaw's technique: he sang through each part, one at a time, until he had mastered it. I tried that for a while and discovered that the best way to hear what was happening in different lines of music together was to sing through one line, and... you guessed it... "play and sing."

Sometimes, I rush so quickly to the "shoes off" moment that I forgot I had work to do. I needed to read and identify the melodies, intervals, and harmonies. I needed to judge the ability of the choir to do the work before taking the shoes off.

Once the shoes come off, connecting with music feels like a special place in my mind. I imagine it being located on the anterior, left side of my head. In that spot, I feel connected to music, choir, and composer. I feel my breath and body becoming a part of the music.

To me, this is where God exists closest to us.

When I go there, the technical problems like wrong notes, diction or phrasing are resolved. If not, the moment vanishes suddenly, jarring me back into a frenzied reality to fix the now broken connection.

Directing the hand bells, chancel choir, or the orchestra, I watch others focused on their part; aware that they're part of a larger whole. I feel like I am surfing a wave. I have no control over that wave, and yet I get to exist in the center of it.

No one ever told me about the little corner that creates music and spins it. I get out of the way, helping to leave the singers alone to artistically make music.

Music making, especially with choirs, is messy. It involves risk and reward. It's always frightening taking the first step into a new, unknown piece. I would imagine starting a new painting must feel similar. When writing each chapter, I want to stay in the world of the previous one, right up until the moment that I escape into the world of the subsequent chapter. When finishing a concert, I go through a period of mourning; that I may never walk through that piece again.

Our shoes protect us from the dangers of creativity, but they also insulate us from the newness and freshness that comes with creation. Once that creation is nearly done, the shoes must come off; just as in the case of new carpeting in a reconstructed building, or figuratively in getting out of the way of artistic music making.

Once our shoes come off, so must our inner critic. Criticism has no place in freshly minted work. Though it may not be the final version that gets cemented in, it's important to let new creativity breathe and grow.

The urge to create needs to be nurtured, and if that means using a simple act to do so, it's an easy choice.

Creativity isn't just about being comfortable, though. Going shoeless involves risk and reward. In the yard, it means feeling the warmth of summer grass, or it can mean stepping over sticks or burrs. In the rehearsal room, it means feeling the tension and release of phrases, but it can also mean pushing the choir to a higher sense of emotion. On the art canvas, it can mean refining a previous section. It can mean trying something new like dancing or playing the piano.

Our shoes, like our egos, protect us from harm. They keep us warm and safe. They both shield us from unnecessary evils. But a creative burst shouldn't be contained by the ego any more than a beach be explored with a pair of shoes. Our egos, ready to protect us by saying "You shouldn't do that," halt our imagination. They stop our exploration of new things; they keep us locked up inside our routines, unable to explore more.

What if we just tried one new thing? What if there were no harm in it? Even fixing a car, composing a song, or making music with others involves dropping our egos for a second and believing that yes, you can do that.

So, for goodness' sake, those creative activities aren't going to accomplish themselves without you. Pack your shoes and go get them!

EPILOGUE

SINGING IN THE MOMENT

What's happening around you right now? At this very moment, what do you see, besides this book? Can you hear the whoosh of air through an a/c vent? How does the chair or the bed you are sitting on feel? Are there any unusual or distinctive smells in the room? How fast is your heart beating? Where are your hands and feet?

Presence – mindfulness – is an art that many of us have found phone apps for, but not many of us practice regularly. It's the art of recognizing that we're right where we need to be.

During these 50 notes, we've talked about planning, working with others, dealing with our own insecurities, looking for answers, and stretching our creativity. But perhaps the most important note is the title.

Sing in the moment.

But why sing?

Singing allows us a second where we make music only for ourselves. It's an experience we can do alone, or together. We don't have to be experts, endure lots of training, or show natural ability to sing.

Singing allows us a time where we might connect with a past memory, a special event, an old experience, or a time long forgotten. When we're singing, we can't talk. We can't participate in other activities. When we sing, we can only sing. So when we sing, we can only experience the current moment in time. If we're reading music, our thoughts are even more focused on the notes, words, and rhythms. If we're good at reading, maybe our minds can focus on the phrasing and musicality too.

But when we're singing, we can't experience the past or future; only what's right in front of us.

Planning is wonderful; reminiscing is wonderful too, but living in this exact moment takes work. We're bombarded by memories of what happened and confronted by tasks that we need to do, but when we sing, we lay all of that aside to focus on the moment. It's the road to contentment and joy.

As you go from here, now having experienced all 50 Notes, remember the most important:

Stay in the moment; it only comes once,

If you have trouble staying in this moment, sing.

Singing in the Moment

THANKS

To Heather McConnell, my sister, who checked the grammar and mechanical problems before allowing me to send the drafts to others.

To Michelle Faught, for copy-editing and proofing, and continually encouraging.

To Anne Guess, who inspired me to continue my writing journey.

To Mary Hupman, for continued encouragement on my writing journey.

To Tiana Pickle, for suggesting that I continue writing these sayings.

To Debbie Rawlins for being a friend through the writing process – making sure the dogs were let out during days I was on writing retreat, taking care of the library items at church so I could write, and making sure I got my details right.

To Sampy Wall, for reading through this set of stories, checking the grammar, and sharing some of his own stories about making music in South Texas with a mutual friend.

To Michael Rebner, my husband, who listened to my stories and gave me inspiration and courage to keep writing.

ABOUT THE AUTHOR

D r. Joel Plaag serves as choir director at Cypress Creek Christian Church in Spring, Texas, where he directs the Cypress Creek Community Chorale, the Cypress Creek Chancel Choir, two handbell choirs, and children's choir. Author of *I'm a Choir Director* and a dissertation on conducting pedagogy, he writes weekly newsletters for the choir, ranging from the sacred to the mundane.

For 17 years, Dr. Plaag taught at colleges before walking away from academia in favor of community choirs and sacred music. His workshops include helping choir directors and developing the spirit through music making. He is married to window designer and senior visual stylist Michael Rebner and together they have two dogs, Teddy, a Great Pyrenees rescue dog, and Freckles, a beagle-corgi mixed breed, found on the street. You can find out more about him at www.joelplaag.cc.

Printed in Great Britain
by Amazon

34532806R00139